IAA 2

MEDIEVAL TOMB TOWERS OF IRAN

Islamic Art and Architecture

Dedicated to the publication of original research
in all aspects of Muslim art and architecture

Volume 1
Abbas Daneshvari, Editor

Essays in Islamic Art and Architecture
(Malibu: Undena Publications, 1981)

Volume 2
Abbas Daneshvari

Medieval Tomb Towers of Iran

Volume 3
Bernard O'Kane

Timurid Architecture in Khurasan
(forthcoming)

MEDIEVAL TOMB TOWERS OF IRAN

An Iconographical Study

By

Abbas Daneshvari

Mazdâ Publishers
In Association With
Undena Publications

انتشارات مزدا

Library of Congress Catalog Card Number: 85-43496

ISBN: 0-939214-34-2

Manufactured in the United States of America

Mazdâ Publishers 1986

In Association With

Undena Publications

Table of Contents

Preface

This book essentially presents my research on the meaning of medieval Persian tomb towers prepared for my doctoral dissertation at UCLA. The present volume is, however, a more detailed and cohesive study of the tomb tower's iconography and departs from many of the conclusions put forth in my dissertation.

I have also omitted from this volume the catalogue of the tomb towers included in the original work. My reasoning for this decision is twofold. Firstly, a majority of these funerary buildings are already published and secondly, Robert Hillenbrand's doctoral dissertation at Oxford on the "Tomb Towers of Iran to 1550" (1974) contains a detailed catalogue of these monuments which preceded my work by more than three years. I look forward to the publication of this volume in the near future.

There are many who have helped me in the preparation of this project. The bulk of my research was accomplished during a trip to Iran in the summer of 1974. This expedition was made possible by a grant from the Social Science Research Council of New York offered to Katharina Otto-Dorn, Gonül Öney and myself. Above all I wish to thank the Council for its support and generosity.

In the many years that I have pondered on and revised the original draft of this manuscript many friends and colleagues have made suggestions that have only changed this work for the better. Foremost among them is Robert Hillenbrand, a trusted friend to whose help and advice I have become accustomed. Bernard O'Kane read and commented on this work during my stay in Cairo in 1981. For his friendship, kindness, encouragement and advice I am always grateful.

Last but not least I would like to thank Katharina Otto-Dorn, the chairperson of my doctoral committee, whose ideas have always been thought provoking and who also read and commented on the content of this manuscript.

D.L. Barlow typed and retyped the many corrected versions of this work. She has been most patient and considerate. My friends Zara Houshmand and Genie Barrett made the drawings. Their talents complement this volume immensely. Joe Coltrane not only typeset this manuscript, but also corrected so many of the typographical errors that I had overlooked. Above all his friendship and kindness was an unparalleled asset in the preparation of this book.

During the years between 1974 and 1977 when I gathered most of the material for this study, one person, Karen Daneshvari, constantly encouraged me to dedicate myself to the completion of this work. Her help, patience, kindness and encouragement have made this book altogether possible. To her I dedicate this volume.

Introduction

> Jābir said: the Messenger of Allah, the peace and blessings of Allah be upon him, forbade the plastering of the grave and the construction of building on it, and sitting on it.[1]

The literary evidence of the ban against raising funerary structures is extensive. All traditions indicate that the Prophet Muḥammad had strictly forbidden the construction of a building on a grave. Veneration of the dead through commemorative structures, lamentations and funerary ceremonies was considered unlawful and was viewed as aspects of the pagan or the Judaeo-Christian heritage. Therefore, in early Islam, there were many attempts to discontinue the pre-Islamic tradition of raising any kind of structure upon a grave. As an example, in al-Bukhārī's *Janā'iz,* Ibn 'Umar orders the removal of a tent from the tomb of 'Abd al-Raḥmān.[2] Likewise, Ibn Baṭṭūṭa (d. 777/1377) writes of Abū Hurayra's strict order that no tent be erected over his grave.[3] The Prophet Muḥammad forbade prayers at his grave by stating that "God slay a people who choose the grave of

1. *A Manual of Ḥadīth,* ed. M.M. 'Alī (Lahore, no date), p. 203. For references to the early traditions cited by Bukhārī, Aḥmad ibn Ḥanbal, Tirmidhī and others on the ban against funerary structures, see K.A.C. Creswell, *The Muslim Architecture of Egypt,* 2 vols. (Oxford, 1952), I:110, note 8 and C.H. Becker, *Christentum und Islam* (Tübingen, 1907), p. 28.
2. *Ṣaḥiḥ al-Bukhārī,* ed. and trans. M.M. Khān (Cantt., 1971), vol. 2:249 and Ignaz Goldziher, "On the Veneration of the Dead," in *Muslim Studies,* 2 vols., ed. S.M. Stern, trans. from German by C.R. Barber and S.M. Stern (Albany, 1977), I:232.
3. *Voyages d'Ibn Batoutah,* Texte Arabe accompagne d'une traduction par C. Defrémery et le dr. B.R. Sanguinetti (Paris, 1853-58), p. 113.

their prophets as mosques."[4] Ibn al-Jauzi (d. 597/1201) writes of the orthodox disapproval of ostentatious graves, the perfuming of graves and the use of ostentatious shrouds.[5] One can cite source after source pointing to this ban against raising a structure (be it a tent or a building) and against elaborate funerary practices in the early Islamic period. Yet in spite of all this, tomb structures became a widespread phenomenon and the doctrine of *"taswīya al-qubūr"* (evenness of the tomb with the surrounding ground) was followed only in the most orthodox of Islamic communities. In fact, Yūsuf Rāghib has shown that despite this ban, commemorative structures were habitually raised for important personages during the earliest Islamic dynasties (the Umayyads and 'Abbāsids).[6] For example, Hārūn al-Rashīd ordered the building of his mausoleum before his death.[7] Strange as it may sound, even the tomb of the Prophet obtained a domed structure, although the strength of orthodox opinion prevented its construction until the thirteenth century.[8]

Considering the extent of this ban, the questions raised on the causes of the perpetuity and popularity of funerary structures are crucial.

A number of scholars have attempted to explain the *raison d'être* of the tomb tower. None, however, have provided

4. Ibn Isḥāq (Ibn Hishām), *Sīrat al-Nabī,* trans. by A. Guillaume as *The Life of Muḥammad* (Oxford, 1970), p. 689; *Idem, Kitāb Sīrat Rasūl Allah,* ed. F. Wüstenfeld (Gottingen, 1859), p. 1021. We also find in al-Bukhārī's *Janā'iz* (cited in Goldziher, I:232) that the Prophet disliked the establishment of mosques over graves. To quote:

> When al-Ḥasan ibn 'Alī expired, his wife pitched a tent on his grave and it remained for one year and then was demolished. They heard a voice saying, 'Have they already found what they lost?' To which a second voice replied: 'No, but they have acquiesced in their fate and have gone away.'

5. *Tablīs al-Iblīs,* partial translation. by D.S. Margoliouth as "The Devil's Delusion" in *Islamic Culture,* XII/4 (1938), pp. 456-7, and the Arabic text ed. M. Munīr (Cairo, 1948), p. 402; see also Robert Hillenbrand, "The Tomb Towers of Iran to 1550," Unpublished dissertation, 2 vols. (Oxford, 1974) II: 113ff.
6. "Les premiers monuments funéraires de l'Islam," *Annales Islamologiques,* IX (1970), p. 21.
7. *Ibid.,* pp. 31-2.
8. Jean Sauvaget, *La mosquée omeyyade de médine* (Paris, 1947), p. 44.

answers that would justify the presence of funerary structures in light of their native Islamic traditions. They have all sought to account for its existence and popularity by establishing a morphological source of influence, preferably outside of the Islamic borders, through which the ritualistic aspects are rationalized.

K.A.C. Creswell, for example, considers the baldachin mausolea of Syria, Palestine and Transjordan (fig. 1) as a source of origin for the canopy tombs of Egypt (i.e. Saba' Banāt at Fusṭāṭ, ca. 400/1010) (fig. 2, plate 1) and subsequently the early square-planned tombs of Iran since he considers the mausoleum of Sāmānid at Bukhārā (fig. 3, plate 2) a stylistic analogue of the Egyptian canopy tombs.[9] Creswell argues that the Syrian canopy tomb was adopted for the earliest mausolea as a compromise between the injunctions of the *ḥadīth* and "a desire to have a monumental tomb." He writes:

> It was probably felt that a tomb under a canopy, open to the sun and wind and rain, did not violate the *ḥadīth* too much. But the need for a miḥrāb soon closed the qibla side and eventually all the remaining sides.[10]

Creswell, however, ignores altogether the problem of the Muslim's "desire to have a monumental tomb." Why was the Islamic culture so eager to violate the *ḥadīth* and its own traditions? Leaving aside the tomb's morphological sources of influence which may or may not be of iconographic significance, the first and most essential question to be asked is what socio-political, cultural or religious forces prompted the Muslims to build tomb towers? Other scholars concerned with the study of tomb towers have attempted,

9. *The Muslim Architecture of Egypt*, I:111-113.
The Syrian and Transjordanian canopy tombs date from the first century B.C. to the third century A.D. Creswell cites two examples, one is from Assar and the other is the mausoleum of Ḥasan Oglu—both dating from the first or the second century A.D. For further examples see the baldachin mausolea of Brad and Dana Nord in North Syria dating from the first to the second century A.D. in E. Will, "La tour funéraire de la syrie et les monuments apparentées" *Syria*, XXVI (1949), plates XIII/2, XIV/1

10. *The Muslim Architecture of Egypt*, I:113.

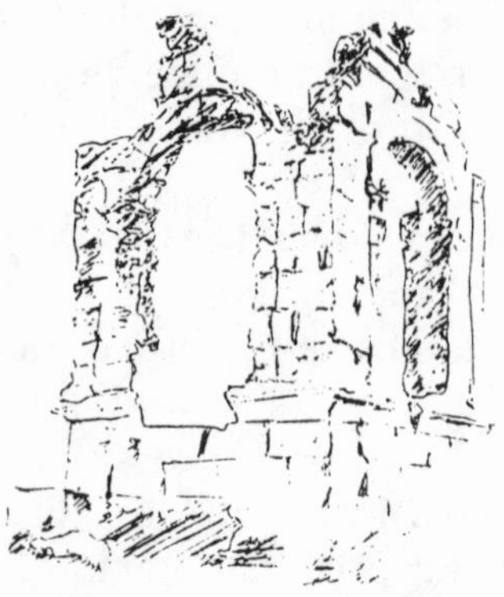

1. *Baldachin mausoleum, Assar, Syria. Circa 3rd. century A.D. After Creswell.*

2. *Saba' Banāt, Fusṭāṭ. Fatimid period. Circa A.D. 1010. After Creswell.*

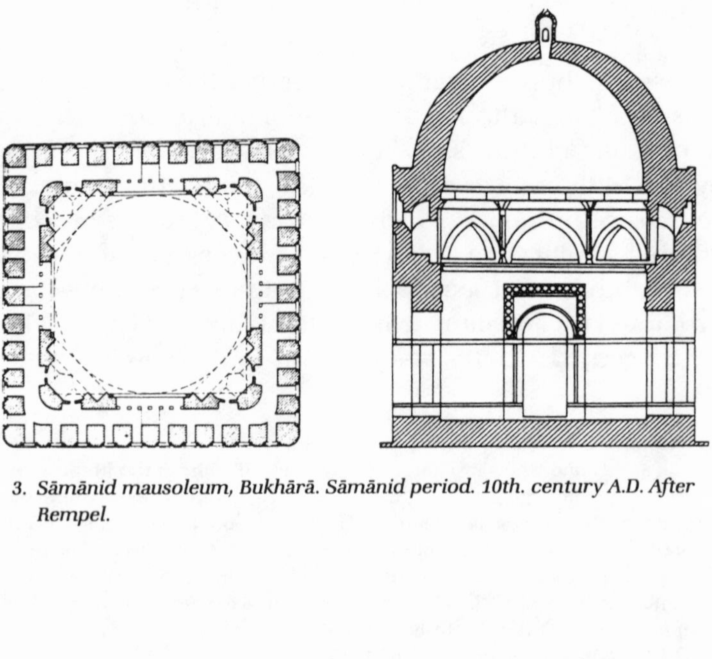

3. *Sāmānid mausoleum, Bukhārā. Sāmānid period. 10th. century A.D. After Rempel.*

like Creswell, to provide some iconographic clues by considering the problems of the tomb structure's stylistic sources of influence. Oleg Grabar considers the significance of the tomb tower in its particular role as a tower of victory and thus ascribes a political meaning across stylistic lines. He writes:

> There a different type of structure, whose symbolic meaning as a memorial, a tower of victory, or a beacon has often been discussed, was used for a funerary architecture, because of its abstract significance as a symbol of power or holiness rather than precisely for any funerary reason.[11]

The theory with the widest circulation considers the tents of Central Asian nomads as an architectural and (even by some of its proponents) an iconographic source for the Islamic tomb tower. Ernst Diez believes that the conically roofed tower was a translation into permanent materials of the royal tent of Central Asian nomads.[12] Similar ideas are expressed by Arthur Upham Pope,[13] Eric Schroeder,[14] S.P. Tolstov,[15] Katharina Otto-Dorn and Emil Esin.[16] Otto-Dorn however, stresses most emphatically, the theory that the morphological sources of the tomb tower account for the tomb structure's iconography. She believes that since the stylistic sources are Central Asiatic then the tomb's meaning too is based upon the funerary rituals of Central Asiatic nomads. She writes in her *L'Art de l'Islam* that the two storey gunbads of Anatolia and western Iran (see for example figs. 4-5) are structural translations of the two-phased

11. "The Earliest Islamic Commemorative Structures, Notes and Documents," *Ars Orientalis*, VI (1966), p. 44.
12. "Principles and Types," *A Survey of Persian Art*, ed. A.U. Pope and P. Ackerman, 14 vols. (Oxford, 1967), III:926. See also Guitty Azarpay, "The Islamic Tomb Tower: A Note on its Genesis and Significance," *Essays in Islamic Art and Architecture in Honor of Katharina Otto-Dorn*, ed. Abbas Daneshvari (Malibu, 1982), pp. 9ff and note 2.
13. "Tents and Pavilions," *Survey*, III:1412.
14. "Seljuk Period," *Survey*, III:1020.
15. *Scythians of the Aral Sea and Khorezm* (Moscow, 1960), p. 358.
16. "Al-Qubbah Al-Turkiyyah: An Essay on the Origins of the Architectonic Form of the Islamic Turkish Funerary Monument," *Atti del Terzo Congresso di Studi Arabi e Islamici, Ravello* (Naples, 1967), pp. 281-313.

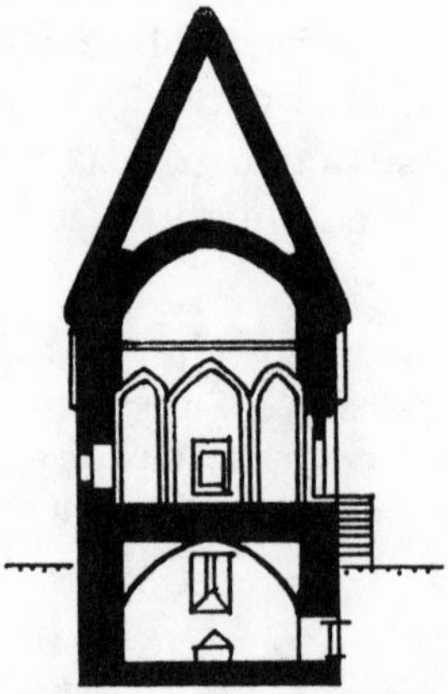

4. *Malik Ghāzī turbah, Kirşehir. Anatolian Saljūq. 11th. century A.D. After Ünsal.*

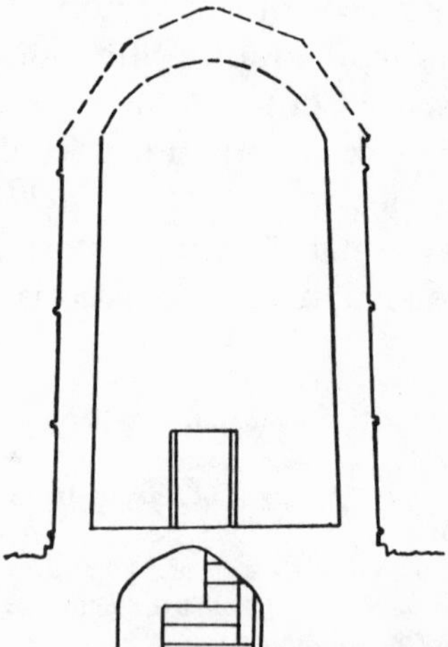

5. *Gunbad-i Shiblī, Damāvand. Saljūq period. 11th. century A.D. After Stronach and Young.*

burial rites among such Central Asiatic nomads as the Huns and the T'ou Kiue.[17] The upper storey, she argues, represents the tent phase of the burial where the body was exposed within a tent and while mourning was expressed through lamentation and circumambulation of the tent. The lower storey, then, would correspond to the second phase of the Central Asiatic burial where the body was buried within a *kurgan*.[18]

Otto-Dorn, therefore, like Creswell, Grabar and others, ascribes a meaning that is derived solely from a study of the tomb tower's morphology and its stylistic analogues.

It is my intention, however, to deal with the iconography of tomb structure in the light of Islamic traditions and perspectives that must have justified its construction despite the ban.

For the iconographic interpretation I have relied upon the historical, religious and literary sources of medieval Iran and, to a lesser extent, of the Arab world, to gain insight into the architectural symbolism of tomb structures. These sources familiarize us with the themes and concepts that were concurrent with the architecture of the period and, after proper examination and scrutiny, reveal facets of funerary architectural iconography in medieval Iran.

What follows is a study of the tomb structure's symbolism on the sacred and profane levels. Although these two concepts are at times overlapping, nevertheless a distinction can be made on the religious and socio-political levels.

On the sacred or the religious plane the tomb mirrors the ontological mutations signaled by death. It expresses a mode of orientation from the physical to the spiritual. Inherent to this transformation is the desire to affirm and establish the ideals of afterlife and the paradisiac purity of the deceased. Moreover, it aims to express the immortality of the soul and the perpetuity of life. We shall see that as a

17. (Paris, 1964), pp. 137-40.
18. Katharina Otto-Dorn, "Figural Stone Reliefs on Seljuk Sacred Architecture in Anatolia," *Kunst des Orients*, XII/1-2 (1978-79), p. 115 and Guitty Azarpay, "The Islamic Tomb Tower," pp. 9-11.

result of these aims the tomb structure is indispensibly fraught with values on the religious, mystical and spiritual planes. These values manifest themselves in the symbolism of the tomb as a heavenly-paradisaic structure and as a shrine.

On the profane level the tomb structure is by its very presence a statement concerning the deceased's social and political importance. It is in fact a message of social and political power aimed at its contemporaries and at posterity.

The Tomb as an Image of Paradise

One factor that was considered important by pre-Islamic and early Islamic peoples was the provision of shade over the grave by the erection of a tent or an edifice for this purpose. This shade—the point is crucial—was sought as a quality of Paradise. We know from the Qur'ān that shade is an aspect of Paradise. Surah 76, verse 14 states that in Paradise,

> The shade thereof is close upon them and the clustered fruits thereof bow down.

And in surah 13, verse 35:

> A similitude of the Garden which is promised unto those who keep their duty (to Allah): Underneath it rivers flow; its food is everlasting, and its shade; this is the reward of those who keep their duty, while the reward of disbelievers is fire.

Surah 36, verses 55-56 reads:

> Lo! Those who merit Paradise this day are happily employed. They and their wives, in pleasant shade, on thrones reclining.

Surah 25, verse 45:

> Hast thou not seen how thy Lord hath spread the shade . . .

This concept of shade as a quality of Paradise also permeates the literary, historical and religious writings of Islam. The examples are abundant. Al-Māfarrukhī describes the gardens of Bikr and Sīāh of Iṣfahān as earthly paradises because of their ample shade.[19] Ḥakīm Samarqandī, taking the idea from the *ḥadīths* of Bukhārī, Tirmidhī, and Muslim, wrote:

> And the Prophet of God, peace and blessings unto him, said: in Paradise there is a tree that if a rider rides beneath its shade for one hundred years he cannot see it end.[20]

It is also important to mention that a number of burial grounds in Islamic Iran were shaded or covered in some way with trees, tents, or buildings. For example, al-Narshakhī writes that *Amīr* Ismāil (d. 279/892) was buried under a huge walnut tree.[21] Many funerary shrines such as the tomb of Jāmī, the Buqʻa-i Tāybād and Gāzūr Gāh in Afghanistan are covered by pistachio trees. Qummī writes that the tomb of Fāṭima, the daughter of the Prophet Muḥammad, was first shaded with leaves.[22] The same author reports two tenth century A.D. burials: one concerns a man by the name of Shajarī who died in Ahwāz and over whose tomb a tent was temporarily erected. Another is about a certain Abū Hāshim who died in his tent and was buried in it.[23] Likewise, ʻAyyūqī writes of a tent burial in his romantic epic *Warqa wa Gulshah* (c. 5/11th century) which is illustrated in a late twelfth or early thirteenth century manuscript (plate 3).[24]

According to al-Yaʻqūbī (d. 279/892) a tent *(fusṭāṭ)* was erected over the grave of ʻAbdullāh ibn ʻAbbās in the mosque of Tā'if.[25] The wife of Imām Ḥasan (d. 1st/7th century) erected

19. Muffaḍḍal ibn Saʻd al-Māfarrūkhī-i Iṣfahānī, *Tarjuma-yi Maḥāsin-i Iṣfahān* (translated into Persian in the year 729/1329 from Māfarrūkhī's Arabic text of 421/1030 by Ḥusaīn ibn Muḥammad ibn Abī al-Riḍā Āwī), ed. ʻA. Iqbāl (Tehrān, 1949), pp. 27-28.
20. *Tarjuma-yi al-Savʻvād-al-Aʻzam* (translated into Persian c. 370/981 by the order of *Amīr* Nūḥ-i Sāmānī) ed. ʻA. Ḥabībī (Tehrān, 1969), p. 82.
21. Abū Bakr Muḥammad ibn Jaʻfar al-Narshakhī (d. 348/959), *Tārīkh-i Bukhārā*, ed. M. Raḍawī (Tehrān, 1972), p. 127.
22. Ḥasan ibn Muḥammad ibn Ḥasan-i Qummī, *Tārīkh-i Qumm* (378/989), trans. from Arabic into Persian by Ḥasan ibn ʻAlī ibn Ḥasan ibn ʻAbd al-Malik Qummī in 805/1403. Ed. S.J. Tehrānī (Tehrān, 1934), p. 213. The Persian word for leaves used by the author is *būryāhā*.
23. *Ibid.*, pp. 234,236.
24. Ed. by Dhabī Allāh-i Ṣafā as *Warqa wa Gulshah-i ʻAyyūqī* (Tehrān, 1966), p. 118.
25. Goldziher, "On the Veneration of the Dead," I:231 and al-Yaʻqūbī *Tārīkh*, ed. M.T. Houtsma, 2 vols. (Leiden, 1883), II:313.

a tent over his grave and maintained it for a year. The tent was later removed due to the Islamic prohibitions against such structures.[26] Likewise, the poet Artāt (d.circa 80/699) erected a tent over the grave of his son ʻAmr and stayed there for a year.[27] We read in Bukhārī's *Janā'iz* about the tent erected over the tomb of ʻAbd al-Raḥmān Abī Bakr[28] and that Abū Hurayra (d. 57/677) forbade the erection of a tent over his grave.[29]

Numerous texts mention burials in mosques and medressehs.[30] A few such as Munshī Kirmānī's *Samṭ al-Ulā Lil-Ḥadrat al-Aūlīyā* are explicit enough to mention that the burial ground was directly beneath the domed chamber of the building.[31] The Prophet Muḥammad was buried inside of a house and the Būyids practiced burials within houses and palace rooms.[32] This practice was so widespread that references to it are found in *Tārīkh-i Bukhārā, Tārīkh-i Nishāpūr, Tārīkh-i Yazd* and *Wafīyāt al-Aʻyān,* to mention just a few.[33]

So far we have seen that shade is an aspect of Paradise and that a great number of tombs were covered or shaded by tents, trees, leaves and permanent edifices. But I have not yet offered any evidence that tomb structures were raised

26. "On the Veneration of the Dead," I:232. See also my note 4.
27. *Ibid.,* I:231 and Abul-Faraj al-Iṣfahānī, *Kitāb al-Āghānī,* 20 vols. (Būlāq, 1868), XI:144.
28. "On the Veneration of the Dead," I:232.
29. *Ibid.,* and my note 3.
30. See for example *Mujmal al-Tawārīkh wa'l-Qiṣāṣ* (520/1126) ed. M. Bahār and and M. Ramaḍānī (Tehrān, 1959), p. 465; *Tārīkh-i Bukhārā,* p. 20 and Muḥammad ibn ʻAlī ibn Sulaymān al-Rawandi's *Raḥatu's-Ṣudūr,* (635/1238), ed. M. Iqbāl, E.J.W. Gibb Memorial, N.S. II (London, 1921), p. 301.
31. Ed. ʻA. Iqbāl (Tehrān 1948), p. 54. This book is a history of Qarā-khitāy in Kirmān between the years 619-703/1223-1306.
32. H. Busse, *Chalif und Grosskönig. Die Bujiden in Irak. Politik, Religion, Kultur und Wissenschaft. 945-1055* (Beirut, 1969), p. 202.
33. *Tārīkh-i Bukhārā,* p. 11; *Tārīkh-i Nishapūr* of Abū ʻAbd Allāh Muḥammad ibn ʻAbdullāh-i Nishapūrī (d. 405/1015), ed. B. Karīmī (Tehrān, 1960), p. 109; *Tārīkh-i Bunakatī* of Fakhr al-Dīn Abū Sulaymān Muḥammad ibn Dāvūd al-Bunakatī (d. 730/1330) ed. J. Shuʻār (Tehrān, 1969), p. 114; *Tārīkh-i Yazd,* written by Jaʻfar ibn Muḥammad ibn Ḥasan-i Jaʻfarī in 732/1333, ed. I. Afshār (Tehrān, 1966), p. 30 and Aḥmad ibn Khallikān's (d. 681/1282) *Wafīyāt al-Aʻyān,* trans. by Baron M. de Slane as *Ibn Khallikān's Biographical Dictionary,* 4 vols. (London and Paris, 1842-70), I:283.

in order to provide shade over the grave, and then to give the tomb a trait of Paradise.

A passage in Bukhārī's *Janā'iz* is significant for it reveals the role of the tomb structure as a provider of shade in the first century of Islam. It states that Ibn 'Umar was angered by seeing a tent *(fusṭāṭ)* upon the grave of Abī Bakr and cried out to his servant: "Remove the tent, because only the pious deeds of the dead will offer him protection and shade."[34] The obvious implication is that the tent (or tomb structure) was placed upon the grave in order to provide the deceased with shade and that this shade was considered to be protective in an esoteric and religious way. Later in the tenth century Qummī writes that the tomb of Fāṭima, the daughter of the Prophet Muḥammad, was originally *shaded* with leaves and acquired a gunbad at a later date.[35] Here again the identical function of shade and gunbad is at least strongly suggested, but the strongest support for our point is Qummī's account of the tomb of a holy shi'ite and a descendant of the Imām Ja'far. He wrote:

> . . . and smallpox spread to his eyes and consequently blinded him. When he died he was buried in the old cemetery of Mālūn. His tomb was a site of pilgrimage and it had *shade* (over it). Then the followers of Khāqān Muflihī came to Qumm in the year 295, and removed the *shade* from his tomb. So the people no longer made pilgrimages to it until some of the wise men of Qumm dreamed in the year 371, that the occupant of the tomb was an exceedingly virtuous man thus pilgrimage to his tomb was a good and highly rewarding deed. Then again his tomb was rebuilt with wood and the people resumed their pilgrimage.[36]

From this account it follows that at least in the earlier periods of Islam the terms shade and tomb structure were

34. "On the Veneration of the Dead," p. 232 and *Janā'iz*, p. 249.
35. *Tārīkh-i Qumm*, p. 213. All of the sources indicate that covering a tomb with leaves was a pre-Islamic custom that was continued into the Islamic period.
36. *Ibid.*, p. 225.

وآبله در چشمش پیدا شد وبدان سبب هر دوچشمش تباه شد. وچون او را وفات رسید او را بمقبره قدیمه بمالون دفن کردند وتربت او را زیارت می کردند وبر سر تربت او سایهٔ بوده است. وچون اصحاب خاقان مفلحی در سنه خمس وتسعین وماتین بقم رسیدند وآن سایهٔ تربت بکشیدند ومدتی زیارت تربت او نمی کردند تا آنکاه که بعضی از ملحای قم بخواب دیدند ودر سنه احدی وسبعین وثلثمائه که ساکن این تربت مردی بسیار فاضل است ودر زیارت کردن تربت او ثواب واجری بسیار است. پس دگر باره بنای قبر او از چوب مجدد گردانیدند ومردم زیارت کردن او سر کرفتند.

used interchangeably, and shade because of its paradisal qualities symbolized protection, relief and even holiness. On its function as protection and relief al-Bukhārī reports in the *Janā'iz* that the Prophet shaded with leaves the tombs of two men who were being tortured so as to provide them with relief.[37] And al-Hujwīrī's description of the funeral of the mystic Dhu'l-Nūn al-Miṣrī in his *The Kashf al-Maḥjūb* indicates the role of shade as an attribute of holiness.

> At his funeral the birds of the air gathered above his bier and wove their wings together so as to shadow it.[38]

Thus, the provision of shade through a tent or a structure presents us with one of the Islamic rationales for the construction of funerary buildings. Furthermore, as our sources have indicated, it is quite clear that the pre-Islamic and early Islamic Arabs were fond of tent burials despite the protestations and objections of the Muslim community's leaders. Clearly, the provision of shade as a protective measure for the soul of the departed far outweighed the more philosophical objections of the learned.

The admitted use of tent-burials among the Arabs also presents us with a definite source of ritualistic influence and a possible morphological source for the later tomb structures. The exact nature of the stylistic influences cannot be determined until more information on the shapes of pre-Islamic and early Islamic Arab tents is brought to light. However, in view of our findings, Ignaz Goldziher's opinion, that it was the Arab tent that was later transformed into a tomb structure appears more plausible than the opinions of those who advocate the influences of Central Asiatic tents on Muslim tomb towers.[39] Although I do not deny stylistic influences from Central Asiatic tents, I must

37. *Janā'iz*, pp. 24-50.
38. 'Alī ibn 'Uthmān al-Jullābī al-Hujwīrī (d. 469/1076), *The Kashf al-Maḥjūb*, ed. and trans. by R.A. Nicholson, E.J.W. Gibb Memorial, N.S. XVII (London, 1970), p. 100. The above story is also found in Sheikh Farīd al-Dīn 'Aṭṭār's (d. 589/1193), *Tadhkirat al-Aūlīyā', ed. M. Iste'lāmī* (Tehrān, 1967), pp. 158-9 and in Abū 'Abd al-Raḥmān Muḥammad ibn Salmī Nīshābūrī's *Ṭabaqāt al-Ṣūfiya* (4/10th century), trans. from Arabic into Persian by Abū Ismāil 'Abdullāh ibn Muḥammad-i Anṣārī (5/11 century), ed. H. Minūchehr (Tehrān, 1966), p. 18.
39. "On the Veneration of the Dead," p. 232.

add that these influences must have been easily admitted due to the analogous beliefs of the Arabs and the Turks with regard to tent burials.[40]

Aside from the shade, another paradisaic quality ascribed to the tomb structure was apparently its ascension toward the heavens. No doubt this ascension was seen as an expression of flight from the earthly to the heavenly or from man to God. The best structural manifestation of this idea can be seen in the Gunbad-i Qābūs which reaches the amazing height of sixty-one meters, while its diameter is only seventeen meters (plate 4, fig. 6). Although most tomb structures have a relatively modest height when compared to the Gunbad-i Qābūs, we can clearly see the importance of a tomb's vertical impetus in our contemporary sources. To quote from Bunākatī's (d. 730/1330) description of the tomb of Ghāzān Khān (d. 1295/1305) (fig. 7):

> (The people) are in wonder (looking) at the tomb of the ruler of the land, (thinking) whether it is a ladder (reaching) to heaven.[41]

In ʿAyyūqī's *Warqa wa Gulshah* the tomb of the lovers, built for them by the king of Syria (Shām), is described as follows:

> The blessed king buried the lovers with his own hands and erected upon their tomb a gunbad that reached up to the heavens.[42]

Similarly, in the *Farhād-nāma* of ʿArif-i Ardibīlī (b. 711/1313) the tomb of Farhād, built by his beloved Shīrīn, is shown as an ascending tower that reaches the dome of the universe:

> Upon his tomb she built a gunbad that reached up to the dome of the heavens.[43]

40. On temporary burials in tents among the nomads of Central Asia see Otto-Dorn, *L'Art de l'Islam*, p. 139; Azarpay, "The Islamic Tomb Tower," pp. 10-12 and W.M. McGovern, *The Early Empires of Central Asia* (Chapel Hill, 1939), p. 33.
41. Dāvūd Bunakatī, *Tārīkh-i Bunakatī*, ed. J. Shuʿār (Tehrān, 1969), p. 466.

زان بنای قبه سلطان ملك در حيرتند　　كين بود آيا مگر بام فلك را نردبان

42. P. 118.

بدست خود آن خسرو بافرين　　دفين كرد او را بزير زمين
كشيد از بر كور شاه جهان　　يكی گنبد سر سوی آسمان

43. Ed. ʿA. Ādhar (Tehrān, 1976), p. 202.

ببالای مزارش گنبدی ساخت　　كه سر برگنبد گردون بر افراخت

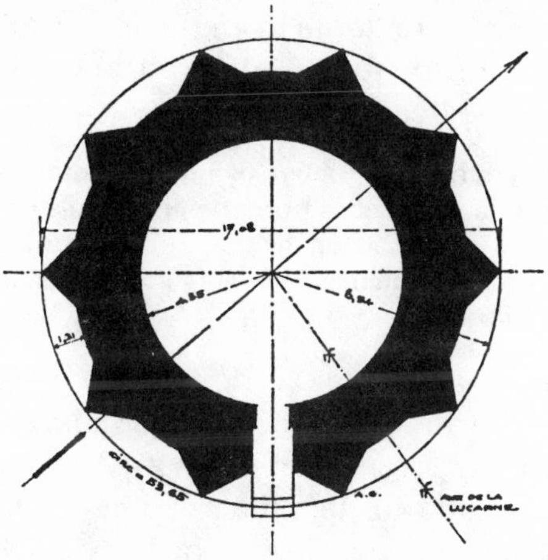

6. *Ground plan of Gunbad-i Qābūs, Gurgān. Ziyārid period. A.D. 1007. After Godard.*

7. *Gunbad-i Ghāzān Khān as reconstructed from Waṣṣāf's description of it. Ghāzānīyya. Il-Khānid period. 14th. century. A.D. After Wilber.*

It is interesting also to quote from the *Vīs wa Rāmīn* (c. 446/1054) of Fakhr al-Dīn Gurgānī where the top of the tower reached up to the heavens (pleiades):

> Then he ordered the construction of a royal dakhma such as was worthy of his fine wife, raised from the fire temple of Burzīn: the top of its tower was built up to the Pleiades. In shape it was redoubtable as a mountain; in ornamentation, fashioned like a gorgeous paradise.[44]

The idea of a tomb structure designed to reach the heavens is also found in a number of other sources and must be viewed as an expression of proximity to God and Paradise. The tower can thus be seen as some kind of ladder or a mountain placing one closer to the heavens. In this light, the glass coffin of the Gunbad-i Qābūs hanging just below the dome can be seen as a further attempt to bring the deceased closer to the heavenly spheres. For in the tradition of the Daīlamites, who were still partial to some of the Zoroastrian beliefs of their ancestors, "closer proximity to the sun brought greater hope of Paradise."[45]

44. Translated by George Morrison (New York, 1972), p. 349. Gurgānī is telling a story set in Parthian times, but his imagery is clearly Islamic. For example, the use of a fire temple for a tomb is a tradition adopted in the Islamic period. For the Parthian origin of Vīs and Rāmīn see V. Minorsky, "Vīs u Rāmīn, A Parthian Romance," *British School of Oriental and African Studies,* XI/4 (1946), pp. 741ff and XII/1 (1947), pp. 20ff.
45. For the Zoroastrian beliefs on the exposure of the body to the sun so that it may have greater hope of Paradise see Mary Boyce, *A History of Zoroastrianism* (Leiden, 1975), p. 113.
Al-Jannabī's report that "Qābūs was buried in a glass coffin with aloes and was hung by chains in the dome of his tomb" must be accepted as true. Robert Hillenbrand ("Tomb Towers of Iran to 1550," I:Qābūs) has suggested that al-Jannabī's correct rendering of the inscription gives credence to the rest of his account. Moreover, Ḥamdallāh-i Mustaufī's (d. 8/14th century) report in his *Tārīkh-i Guzīda* (ed. and tr. E. G. Browne and R.A. Nicholson, Gibb Memorial Series, 14, nos. 1-2, [London, 1911], p. 425) that the coffin of the Būyid *vizīr* Sāhab-i 'Ibbād was hung from the ceiling of his house while the mourning dignitaries paid their respects gives further credence to al-Jannabi's account of Qābūs' coffin (This story is also cited in *Ḥabīb al-Siyar* and in Sheila S. Blair, "The Octagonal Pavilion at Natanz: A reexamination of Early Islamic Architecture in Iran," *Muqarnas,* ed. Oleg Grabar, I (1983) pp. 88-89). For *Ḥabīb al-Siyar* see *A History of the Minor Dynasties of Persia Being an Extract from Ḥabīb-us-Siyār of Khundamīr,* ed. G.S.A. Ranking (London, 1910), p. 112.

This concept of verticality as a sign of grandeur and proximity to Paradise is also found in secular architecture. Al-Hamdānī's early tenth century text translated as the *Antiquities of South Arabia* describes the palace of Ghumdān in Yemen as "Twenty stories high the palace stood, flirting with the stars and the clouds. If Paradise lies over the skies, Ghumdān borders on Paradise."[46]

Likewise, the sufi literature provides us with its own parallel. Among the sufis the "polar dimension" is an ascending direction defining the allegorical East (Orient). The East (Orient) is ultimately the eighth clime and thus Paradise. Henry Corbin writes on this point:

> This Orient is not comprised in any of the seven climes *(keshvars);* it is in fact the eighth clime. And the direction in which we must seek this eighth clime is not on the horizontal but on the vertical. This suprasensory, mystical Orient, the place of the Origin and of the Return, object of the eternal Quest, is at the heavenly pole; it is the pole at the extreme north, so far off that it is the threshold of the dimension "beyond." . . . Only an ascensional progress can lead toward this cosmic north chosen as a point of orientation.[47]

The Symbolism of Plan-Types

An important question is whether or not the designers of the gunbads meant to express any beliefs by choosing specific shapes for their structures. The question, of course, does not imply that every tomb structure was planned and erected with a given meaning in the mind of its builders. We must take into account that designs were adopted and continued from a purely traditional and practical point of view as well. However, some sources suggest that *some* of the shapes chosen for tomb stuctures were rich in paradisaic symbolism. This symbolism may either have accounted for the design of the structure or may have been ascribed to it at a later date.

The extant plan-types up to the end of the Il-Khānid period are:

46. Oleg Grabar, *The Formation of Islamic Art* (New Haven, 1973), p. 79.
47. Henry Corbin, *The Man of Light in Iranian Sufism,* trans. by Nancy Pearson (Boulder and London, 1978), p. 2.

1. The square: a cubical body with four entrances, crowned by a dome (with one entrance in its later variations)(figs. 3,8; plates 2,5).

2. The circular: a cylindrical body topped by a dome which may be covered by a cone (variations of this plan have vertical flanges)(figs. 6,9,10; plates 4,6,7).

3. The hexagonal: the few extant examples of these structures are in such a state of ruin that their dating is quite problematic and thus no conclusions on their meanings can be reached. The extant examples are the Pīr-i Murād at Tūrānpusht, Géza Fehérvári's find at Qubeyrā in Kirmān and the one found by Kleiss at Kāj, Iṣfahān (fig. 13).[48]

4. The octagonal: an eight-sided body crowned by a single or double dome (the outer dome may also be semicircular) (figs. 11,12,13; plates 8-10).

5. The decagonal: a ten-sided drum crowned by an inner dome and an outer cone)(fig. 14, plate 11).

6. The twelve-sided (fig. 7).

Among square tombs, the earliest extant example is the Sāmānid tomb at Bukhārā which has a cubical body with four entrances and is crowned by a dome.[49] Later variations of this plan eliminate three of these entrances, mostly in favor of interior and/or exterior niches. This type of structure is closely related to fire temples *(chāhār-ṭāq)* of the Sassanian period.

48. Géza Fehérvári and A.D.H. Bivar, "Qobeyrā 1974: Advance Report on the Third Session," *Proceedings of the Third Annual Symposium on Archeological Research in Iran,* (Tehrān, 1975), p. 258. For Pīr-i Murād see Iraj Afshār, Yādgārhā-yi Yazd, 3. vols. (Tehrān, 1966), p. 562. The hexagonal structure at Kāj is published by Wolfram Kleiss, "Bericht über Erkundsfahrten in Iran im Jahre 1971," *Archaeologische Mitteilungen aus Iran,* 5 (1972), p. 220, Abb. 94.

49. Similar tenth century tomb structures, with minor variations, were common in Central Asia. A photograph of Imām Bab Cemetary at Merv (end of tenth century), now destroyed, shows a domed cube with four entrances. Other tombs showing variations of this design are: domed cubes with three entrances and one miḥrāb (anonymous mausoleum at Chahr Juy), two entrances (mausoleum of Aḥmad), and one entrance with the remaining three walls deeply recessed on the interior (Kizbibi near Merv). The information on these mausoleums was derived from Oleg Grabar's "The Earliest Commemorative Structures, Notes and Documents," *Ars Orientalis,* IV (1966), p. 21. Also see G.A. Pugachenkova, *Puti Razvitiya Arkhitekturi Iuzhonogo Turkmenistana Pori Rabovladeniya Feodalizma,* in *Trudi Iuzhno Turkmenistanskoi Arkheol. Ekspeditsky,* VI (Moscow, 1958).

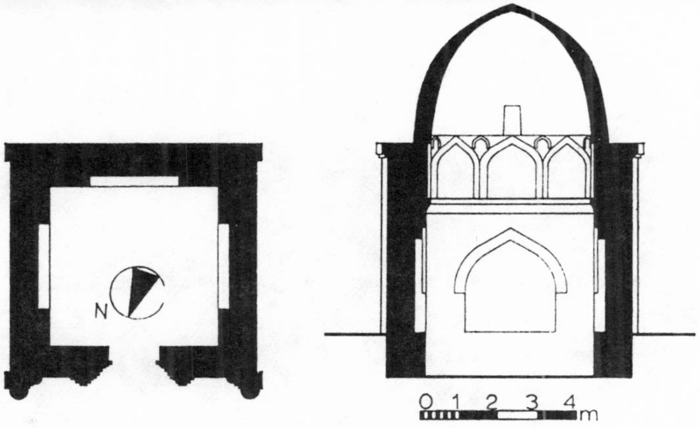

8. Pīr masoleum, Tākistān. Saljūq period. 12th. century A.D. After After Kleiss.

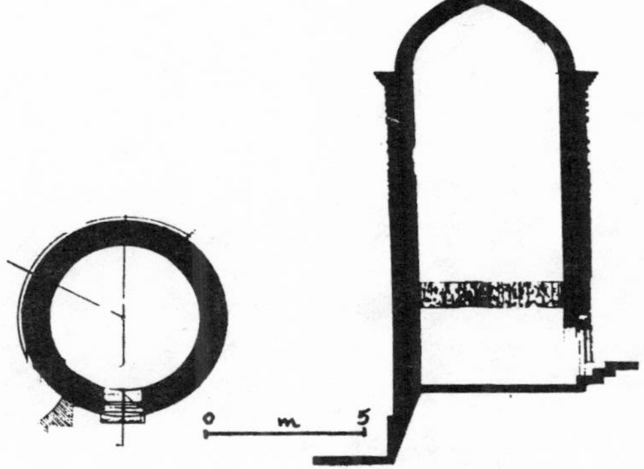

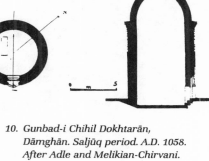

9. Gunbad-i Pīr-i 'Alamdār, Dāmghān. Ghaznavid period. A.D. 1021. After Adle and Melikian-Chirvani.

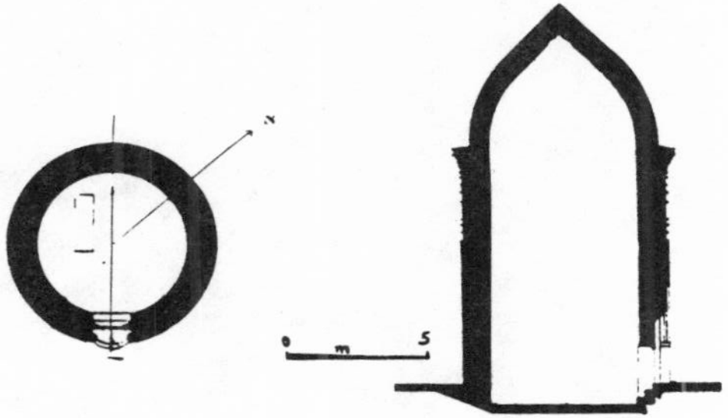

10. Gunbad-i Chihil Dokhtarān, Dāmghān. Saljūq period. A.D. 1058. After Adle and Melikian-Chirvani.

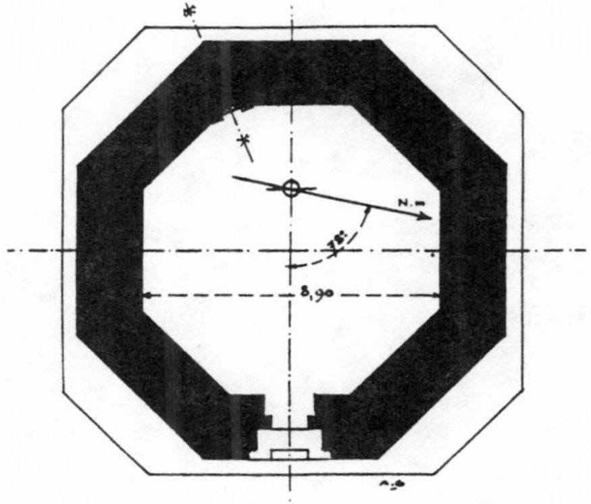

11. Ground plan of Gunbad-i 'Alī, Abarqū. Kākūyid period. A.D. 1038. After Godard.

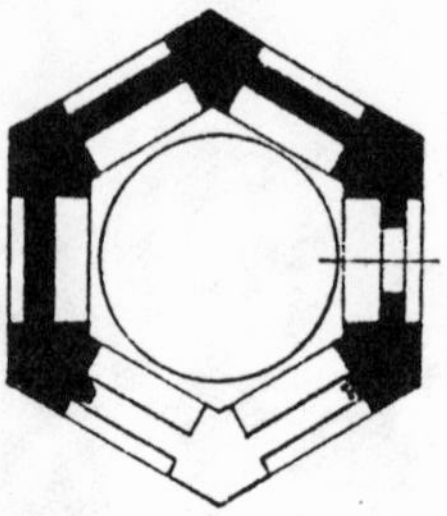

13. Remains of the six-sided tomb at Kāj. Unknown date. After Kleiss.

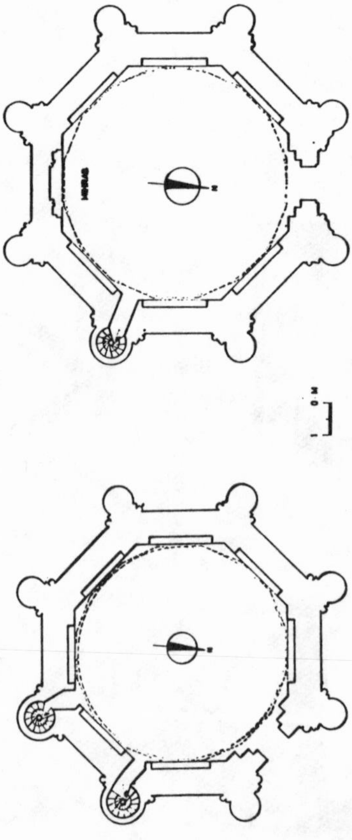

12. Towers I and II of Kharraqān, Kharraqān. Saljūq period. A.D. 1067-8 and 1093-4. After Stronach and Young.

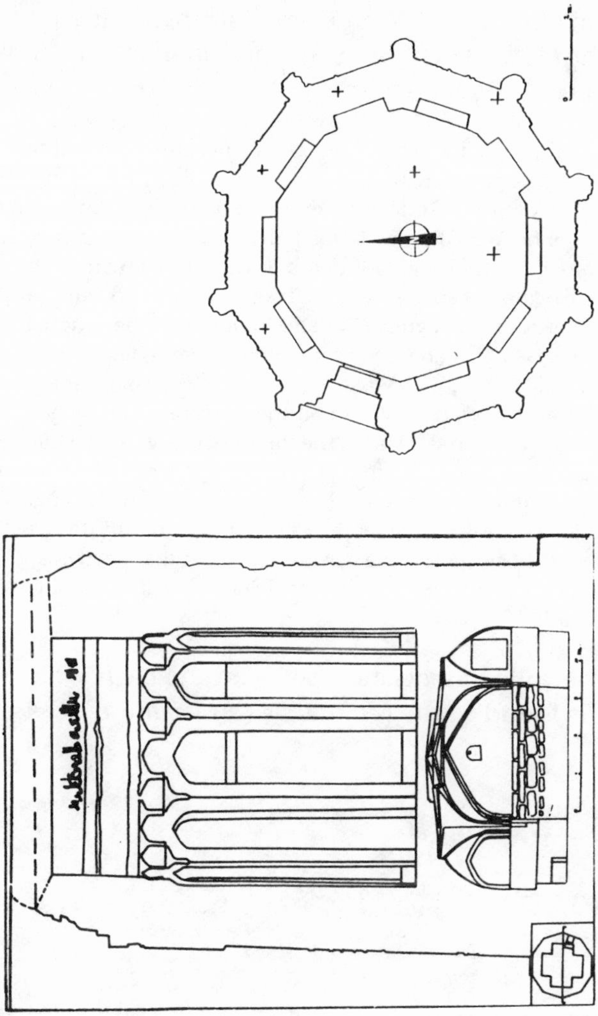

14. Gunbad-i Kabūd, Marāgha. Saljūq period. Aḥmadilī period. A.D. 1197. After Daneshvari.

The Sassanian fire temple was a holy structure by virtue of its function and incorporated religious symbolism. Did the *chāhār-ṭāq* have any meaning in the Islamic period, or was it merely a blind continuation of an earlier design? A passage in Qummī's *Tārīkh-i Qumm* strongly suggests that the *chāhār-ṭāq* had paradisaic symbolism in Islamic Iran of the tenth century. He wrote:

> So says Abū Muqātil: I heard from Abī al-Ḥasan Abī ibn Muḥammad, peace be upon him, that on the night of the Mi'rāj, when the Prophet, the praise of God be upon him and his family, was being taken to the heavens, he saw in *the fourth heaven a dome of light that had four columns and four doors.* It was like a green silk brocaded with gold because it was so fresh, verdant and pure. And when the eyes of the Rightly Guided Muḥammad, the Prophet of God, the praise of God be upon him and his family, fell upon that dome, he said: "O Gabriel, what is this dome, for I have not seen one better and more beautiful in all the heavens." Gabriel, peace be upon him, answered: "This is the image of a city called Qumm. Here, from among the servants of God will gather the faithful to await your coming on the day of resurrection and reckoning, so that you intercede on behalf of the religious community. Here will also gather the faithful and the devout to await Muḥammad (Mahdī) for intercession on behalf of the friends of the family of Muḥammad . . ."[50]

A more explicit association between the *chāhār-ṭāq* and Paradise is found in the *Mujmal al-Tawārīkh wa'l Qiṣāṣ,* an

50. Pp. 96-7.
ابو مقاتل گوید که از ابی الحسن علی بن محمد علیهما السلام شنیدم که شب
معراج که رسول صلی الله علیه وآله وسلّم را بآسمان بردند در آسمان چهارم
نظر کرد بقبهٔ از نور که آنرا چهار رکن بود بچهار در گوشیا استبرق سبز بود
از خرّمی وسبزی و پاکی و تازگی چون نظر صایب محمد رسول الله صلی الله علی وآله
وسلّم بر آن قبّه آمد فرمود که ای جبرئیل این چه قبّه ایست؟ که من در همه
آسمان مثل ومانند و بهتر و نیکوتر ار آن ندیدم. جبرئیل علیه السلام گفت که این
صورت شهریست که آنرا قم گویند که ازبند کان خدای از مومنان در آن جمع شوند
وانتظار توکشند از برای قیامت وحساب تا تو شفیع امّت کردی وهم چنین مومنان
وزاهدان در آن جمع شوند وانتظار محمّد (مهدی) کشند وشفاعت کردن او درباره
دوستداران آل محمّد ...

In Christian art the cubical shape with a dome was a cosmological shape. See V. Strika, "The Turbah of Zumurrud Khātūn in Baghdad, Some Aspects of the Funerary Ideology in Islamic Art," *Annali dell'Instituto Orientale di Napoli,* 38, N.S. XXVIII (1978), p. 293; G. Baltrusaitis, *Cosmographie chrétienne dans l'art du moyen age* (Paris, 1939); A.C. Soper, "The Dome of Heaven," *Art Bulletin,* XXIX (1947), pp. 225-248 and W. Wolska, *La topographie chrétienne de Cosma Indicopleustes* (Paris, 1962), pp. 113ff.

anonymous work dating from 520/1126. Here too the *chahār-ṭāq* is found on the fourth level of the heavens which is the domicile of the sun. The story begins with our hero Ḥāmid ibn Khalīl Ibrāhīm receiving guidance from 'Umrān ibn al-'Ays ibn 'Ishāq in his search for the source of the river Nile, one of the four rivers flowing from Paradise. 'Umrān instructs him about the levels of Paradise by identifying each layer with a metallic substance. The fourth level, the domicile of the sun, is naturally identified with gold.

> As (you journey) you will reach a land where the mountain and the plain are made of iron. When you pass this you will come to a land where the mountain, trees and the plain are made of brass. After this you will arrive at a land where everything, as far as the eye can see, is made of silver. *Then you will come to the land of gold: there you shall come to a place where there is a lofty edifice with a dome. it has four doors and is all golden.* There you must descend, for it is the source of the water. So Ḥāmid left and did as he was instructed. He reached the place and saw wonders: the rampart from which the water flowed, and (he saw) the golden dome with water flowing from its four doors. Three streams of water disappeared into the ground while the one that flowed over it was the source of the river Nile. Ḥāmid drank from the (Nile's) water and rested. Then he tried to ascend the wall (but) the angel cried: "Stop, O Ḥāmid, for you have reached the utmost extremity of the Nile. And it is Paradise whence the water flows . . ."[51]

51. Pp. 474-5.

چون (بروی) بزمینی رسی وکوه وصحرا همه آهنین بینی چون بگذشتی بزمینی رسی
وهرچند چشم کار کند و از آن پس بزمین زر رسی که دیواری بینی وقبه وشرفها
همه زرین وآنرا چهار در وآنجا فرود آئی که آب از انجاه بیرون می آید. پس
حامد برفت وهمچنان کرد تا بجائی رسید و آن عجایب دید که آب از آن سور
بیرون میاید و در آن قبه زرین و از آن چهار در همی بیرون آمد وسه شاخ در
زمین نا پیدا گشت ویکی بر زمین میرفت وآن اصل رود نیل بود وحامد از آن
بخورد وبیاسود وخواست که بر بالای آن سور رود وفریشته آواز داد که بایست
یاحامد که بغایب منتها نیل رسیدی واین بهشت است که از آنجا همی فرود آید.

It is interesting to note that the water flows down from the dome of the *chahār-ṭāq* described by the angel as the highest level of Paradise. This imagery of the *chahār-ṭāq* as the source of the water brings to mind Ibn al-Balkhi's description of the Gunbad-i Kīrman in the Sassanian city of Firūzābād which may indicate a pre-Islamic tradition for our myth. He wrote that the Gunbad-i Kīrman had four stone walls and was topped by a brick dome. Water was piped from one *farsang* away and spouted forth from the summit of its dome. *Fārs-nāma* (6/12 century) ed. by G. Le Strange and R.A. Nicholson (London, 1968), p. 138.

This narrative is a classic tale of celestial ascent through the vertical levels of Paradise.[52]

What we have in these two passages is a description of the *chāhār-ṭāq* as a symbol of the fourth level of Paradise. The question now is, what is the significance and the meaning of this level?

Firstly it is the domicile of the sun and thus a source of light.[53] The fourth level is therefore always radiant. In al-Hujwīrī's description of the stations of the spirit, the fourth station (an allusion to the fourth level of Paradise) is identified with lamps of light hanging from the throne of God.[54] Or as we have just seen in Qummī's *Tārīkh-i Qumm* and *Mujmal al-Tawārīkh* the fourth level is identified with light and gold.[55] However, more important than the identification of the fourth level with sun and light is its designation as the domicile of the devout and religious. In al-Hujwīrī's terms this level is the station of the *ahl-i minān* or the beneficient.[56] In Qummī's account the fourth level is the gathering place of the devout and faithful.[57] In *Miṣbāh al-Arwāḥ by* Kirmānī (7/13th century) the fourth level is "... the home of the devout and the resting place of the warriors of happiness ... The people of this city, whether learned or not, are all devout and religious."[58]

Thus, considering the symbolism of the *chāhār-ṭāq* as the fourth level of Paradise and as the home of the devout and the religious, its adoption for a tomb is quite appropriate.

In an elegy written by the Il-Khānid poet Sa'īd Harawī, the *chāhār-ṭāq* is described as a universal, heavenly and everlasting structure. He wrote:

52. See for example Avicenna's (Abū 'Alī Sīnā, d. 428/1036) *Risālat al-Ṭayr* in Henry Corbin's *Avicenna and the Visionary Recital,* pp. 186-192 and Shams al-Dīn Muḥammad Bardsīrī Kirmānī, *Miṣbaḥ al-Arwāḥ* (7th/13th century), ed. B. Furūzānfar (Tehrān, 1970), pp. 44-64.
53. *Tārīkh-i Qumm,* p. 967; *Miṣbāḥ al-Arwāḥ,* p. 4950.
54. *The Kashf al-Maḥjūb,* p. 265.
55. See notes 50-51 and their accompanying texts.
56. *The Kashf al-Maḥjūb,* p. 265.
57. *Tārīkh-i Qumm,* p. 00.
58. PP. 49-50. See note 53.

گفتا که مقام زاهدانست وآرامگه مجاهدانست

اهلش چه عوام وچه معارف یکسر همه عابدند وزاهد

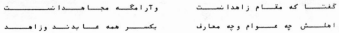

> It is deserving of the earth if the heavens cry blood upon it, or if the world mourns stormily from ocean to ocean ... We are far from him, but the angels have placed the altar of his veneration in the *Chaḥār-Ṭāq-i Lā-makān.*[59]

To conclude, clearly the *chaḥār-ṭāq* was fraught with heavenly and paradisaic symbolism in Islamic Iran. It signified the fourth level of Paradise and the resting place of the devout and religious. It was, therefore, a fitting plan for a tomb since it envisioned the Paradise sought after death.

The circular planned tomb towers with their cylindrical bodies and, in most cases, conical roofs, were quite popular in the northern and central regions of Iran. For the most part, the earlier structures have simple cylindrical elevations while only a few show triangular flanges on their drums such as Gunbad-i Qābūs (fig. 6, plate 4), Gunbad-i Mihmān-dūst (fig. 15, plate 12) and Burj-i Ṭughril (fig. 16, plate 13). By the time of the Mongolian period, however, these flanges are found on a greater number of tomb structures as seen in ʿAbdallāh-i Varāmīn (plate 14), Rādekān East (plate 15) and Basṭām (plate 16).

I regret that I cannot as yet provide with certainty any answers to the iconography of these flanges. They may be purely structural or perhaps are devices used to emphasize the vertical ascension of the tower, or, they may have alluded to heavenly bodies: especially in the case of Shams al-Maʿālī whose name means the "Sun of the Heights," the heavenly configuration of the structure may be a reference to his name. The fact that the tower bears the date in solar calendar gives some credibility to this thought particularly when we consider the importance of the sun in the Daīlamite traditions.

59. Saʿīd Harawī's poem is left to us in the anthology of *Munis al-Aḥrār fī Daqāʾiq al-Ashʿār* compiled by Muḥammad ibn Badr al-Jājarmī in 741/1341. Ed. Mīr Ṣāleḥ Ṭabībī, 2 vols. (Tehrān, 1968), II:820.

ما از او دوریم گرچه قدسیان بنهاده اند
منبر تعظیم او در چهار طاق لا مکان

Lā-makān means of no specific place, universal, everlasting and heavenly. On the meaning of *lā-makān* see *Farhang-i Dihkhudā,* s.v. "*lā-makān.*"

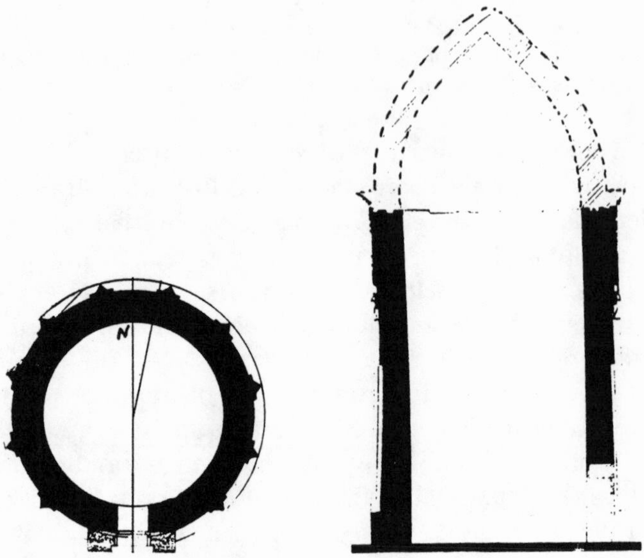

15. Gunbad-i Mihmāndūst, Dāmghān. Saljūq period. A.D. 1097. After Adle and Melikian Chirvani.

16. Burj-i Ṭughril, Rayy. Saljūq period. A.D. 1139. After Coste.

In any event, the paradisaic significance of the cylindrical tower with the conical roof is brought across in a passage found in Rashīd al-Dīn's (d. 716/1317) *Jāmī' al-Tawārīkh* and repeated in *Tārīkh-i Bunākatī*. These passages describe the death of Hulā Kū Khān, the first Il-Khānid ruler of Persia who ruled from 1256 to 1265. I quote from *Tārīkh-i Bunākatī* since the text is better preserved.

> . . . When the year of the Cow arrived, in the month of Rabī' al-Ākhar of the year 663, (Hulā Kū Khān) became ill. During that time there appeared every night a comet in the shape of a cylinder with a cone and as this comet disappeared (Hulā Kū) died on Sunday night, the nineteenth of Rabī' al-Ākhar.[60]

Clearly this image, formed by the light of the heavenly stars, has the shape and the function of a tomb structure. It in fact appears as a heavenly archetype of an earthly tomb signaling Hula Ku's predestined fate.[61]

We come now to the octagonal type of tomb structures. The Gunbad-i 'Alī from 448/1016-7 is the earliest dated octagonal gunbad of Muslim Iran (fig. 11, plate 8) However, recent excavations and restorations conducted by the Iṣfahān Office of the National Organization for the Protection of the Ancient Monuments have revealed that the octagonal Pavilion at Naṭanz was built during the Būyid period (389/999) and is thus the earliest dated dome in central Iran (fig. 17, plate 17).[62] Sheila Blair considers this structure to be in all likelihood a mausoleum and therefore provides for the Iranian world a direct link between Qubbat al-Sulaybiya

60. P. 425; see also Rashīd al-Dīn's *Jāmī al-Tawārīkh*, ed. M. Bahār and M. Ramaḍānī, 2 vols. (Tehrān, 1940), II:736.

وچون سال گاو در آمد واقع در ربیع الاخر سنه ثلث وستین وستمائه (٦٦٣) رنجور شد ودر آن زمان ذو ذوابهٔ مثل استوانه مخروط ظاهر شد وهر شب پیدا می گشت و چون آن ذو ذوابه ناچیز شد در شبِ یکشنبه نوزدهمِ ربیع الاخر مذکور وفات یافت.

61. I should point out here that the circle has always been associated with the heavens because of the circular motion of astral bodies. To quote from Sanā'ī's (Ḥakim Abu'l-Majd Majdud, d. 547/1152) *Ḥadīqatu'L-Ḥaqīqat,* [ed. and trans. by Major J. Stephenson (New York, 1972), pp. 37-8]: "He made a *wheel* of pure emerald and on the wheel He bound silver jars (stars); He caused a candle (sun and moon) and the candlestick (sky) to revolve in the heavens in the path of the ignoble."

62. Sheila S. Blair, "The Octagonal Pavilion at Natanz: A Reexamination of Early Islamic Architecture in Iran." *Muqarnas,* ed. Oleg Grabar, I (1983), pp. 69ff.

(251/865) and the later Iranian octagonal tomb structures (fig. 18).[63] This point is crucial for determining the iconography of the early octagonal tomb towers in Iran.

The meaning of Qubbat al-Sulaybiya can be understood in the light of its relations to the Christian/Byzantine world of imagery and iconography.[64] Its plan is based upon the designs of Christian Martyria and Baptesteria, whose octagonal plans stood for Paradise, life everlasting and harmony.[65] The Muslims were of course most receptive to this shape and its paradisaic meanings, for in Muslim eschathology and cosmology the concept of Paradise is expressed as eight gardens with eight doors. The names of these gardens which are derived from the Qur'ānic descriptions of Paradise are: *Dār al-Salām, Jun'nat al-Ma'wī, Jun'nat al-'Adan, Jun'nat al-Firdaus, Dār al-Qarār, Jun'nat al-Na'īm, Jun'nat al-Khuld,* and *Dar-i Raḥmat.* These eight paradises comprise the sphere of the fixed stars (*Kursī,* Firmament) and everyone according to his merit attains a level on this ascending order of Paradise. The highest level is the eighth sphere located beyond Saturn. To quote from 'Aṭṭār's (d. 589/1193) *Haylāj-nāma:*

> If thou comest to our religion,
> thou wilt pass beyond the seventh heaven.[66]

63. *Ibid.*
64. If these Christian influences were not handed down directly then they were channeled through such intermediaries as Qubbat al-Sakhra in Jerusalem. For a discussion of Christian-Byzantine influences on the Dome of the Rock see K.A.C. Creswell, *A Short Account of Early Muslim Architecture* (Beirut, 1968), pp. 35-40 and Oleg Grabar, "The Umayyad Dome of the Rock in Jerusalem," *Ars Orientalis,* III (1959), 33-62. See also V. Strika, "The Turbah of Zumurrud Khātūn in Baghdad, Some Aspects of Funerary Ideology in Islamic Art," *Annali dell' Instituto Orientale di Napoli,* 38, N.S. XXVIIII (1978), pp. 293ff.
65. The symbolism of the octagon in Christian art is well known and is discussed in a majority of publications dealing with this topic. However, for an excellent and intelligent discussion of the meaning of the octagon and especially the octagonal plan of S. Vitale in Ravenna see O.V. Simson, *The Sacred Fortress* (Chicago, 1948), pp. 50ff.
66. In Fritz Meier's "The Spiritual Man in the Persian Poet 'Aṭṭār," *Spiritual Disciplines,* trans. by Ralph Manheim (New York, 1970), p. 269.

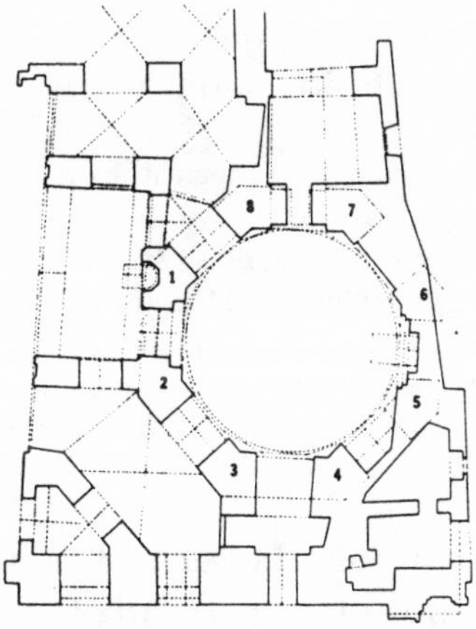

17. The Octangonal Pavilion, Naṭanz. Būyid period. A.D. 999. After Blair.

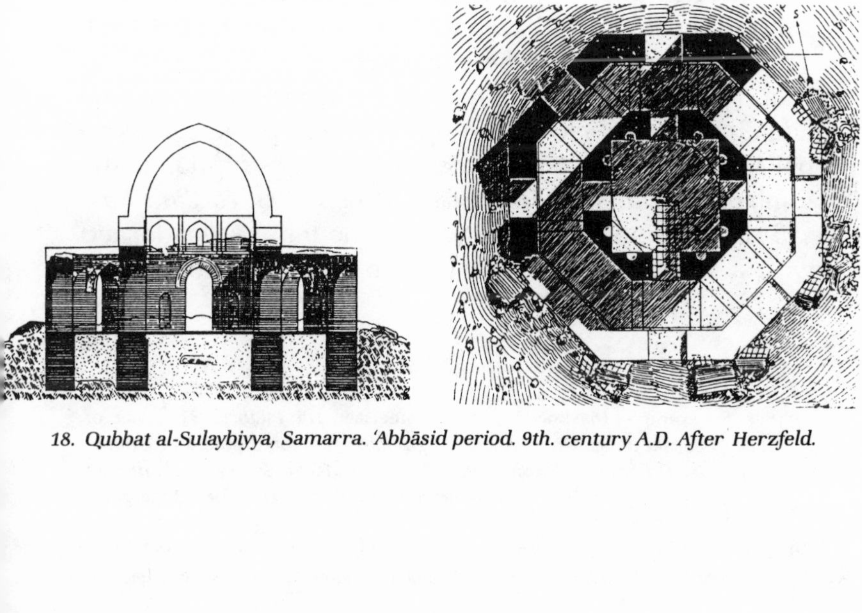

18. Qubbat al-Sulaybiyya, Samarra. 'Abbāsid period. 9th. century A.D. After Herzfeld.

The Muslims thus viewed number eight as a symbol of Paradise. A passage from Ḥakīm Abūl-Majd Majdūd-i Sanā'ī's (d. 547/1152) *Ḥadīqat-u'l-Ḥaqīqat* demonstrates the symbolism of the number eight in Islam:

> When suddenly there comes on thee thy appointed time, and the things of the world all pass away, and the two hands and feet fail in their office, to thee in thy helpless state he gives an exchange for these four. Hands and feet are shut up in the tomb, and eight heavens become thy fortune; eight doors are opened to thee, virgins and the youths of Paradise can come before thee, that going joyfully to any door thou wilst mayest lose remembrance of this world.[67]

This quote, interesting also because of its funerary context, implies the translation of the concept of the eight gates into an architectural form. There is of course concrete evidence of this architectural translation in the later periods when some octagonal structures were called *hasht bihisht* (eight paradises) as in *hasht bihishts* of Uzūn Ḥasan (891/1486) and those built at Tabrīz, Herāt and Iṣfahān.[68]

We know of a few twelve-sided tomb structures. To mention two examples: Rādekān East, built circa 1280-1300 (plate 15); and the tomb of Ghāzān Khān, built between 1297-1304. This plan-type should be considered Il-Khānid since no Saljūq or earlier examples have as yet been found. The only clue, but an explicit one, to the heavenly paradisaic symbolism of this plan-type comes from the description of the tomb of Ghāzān Khān in Waṣṣāf's (d. 698/1299) *Tārīkh-i Waṣṣāf.* He mentions that each wall of the tomb was adorned with a sign of the zodiac.[69] These signs, as the obvious

67. Tr. Stephenson, p. 21.

68. See, for example, Ingeborg Luschey-Schmeisser, *The Pictorial Tile Cycle of Hasht Behesht in Iṣfahān and Its Iconographic Tradition* (Rome, 1978), pp. 1-3 and Lisa Golombek, "From Tamerlane to Taj Mahal, *Essays in Islamic Art and Architecture, in Honor of Katharina Otto-Dorn,* ed. Abbas Daneshvari (Malibu, 1982), p. 47.

69. Sharaf al-Dīn Waṣṣāf, *Tārīkh,* ed. 'A. Āyatī (Tehrān, 1967), p. 230 and Wilber, *The Il-Khānid Period, p. 126. Eric Schroeder (Survey,* III:1020) speculates that

symbols of the heavens, point out the heavenly iconography of this twelve-sided tomb structure (fig. 7).

The problems of the meaning of the hexagonal and the decagonal structures must remain to be solved when further information is brought to light on them.

It is, therefore, important to point out that a majority of the plan-types of tomb towers such as the square, cylindrical, octagonal and the twelve-sided indicate a heavenly-paradisial significance and may thus have been viewed as earthly forms of heavenly archetypes. On this latter note it is appropriate to end this chapter with the following quote from Bunākatī's *Tārīkh* where a direct correlation between an earthly and heavenly cylindrical funerary tower is established.

> ... And when (Shāmkūni's) life came to an end, there suddenly appeared in that city a glass gunbad. Shāmkūni went into that gunbad and slept like a lion. People could see him from the outside ... And suddenly they saw a light in the shape of a cylinder leaving from the top of his gunbad.[70]

The Entrance Panel

The entrance panels of tomb structures, like those of mosques and madrasas, had a standard design. Each panel consisted of one or more rectangular frames enclosing the arches of the niche. Looking at contemporary miḥrābs we see a strong relationship between these two forms (compare figs. 19-20 with figs. 21-23). This relationship does not appear to be accidental due to a number of factors such as

---

the twelve-sided towers may reflect the sacred number of Imāmites. This is a possibility if the structure's twelver shi'ite patronage can be established.

70. P. 330.

وجون مدت حیات او باخر رسید در آن شهر گنبدی از بلور صافی یکباره آفریده شد. شامکونی در آن گنبد رفت و همچو شیر بخفت واز بیرون گنبد خلایق اورا می دیدند ... ناگاه نوری دیدند مانند استوانه روشن که از سر گنبد بیرون رفت.

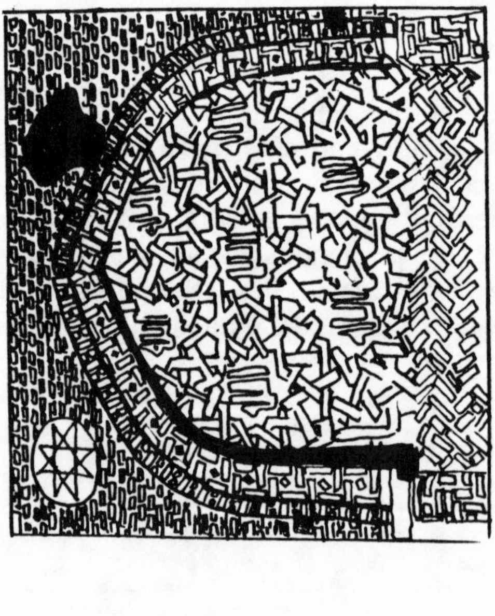

19. *Detail of Kharraqān I entrance, Kharraqān. Saljūq period. A.D. 1067-8. After a photo in Stronach and Young.*

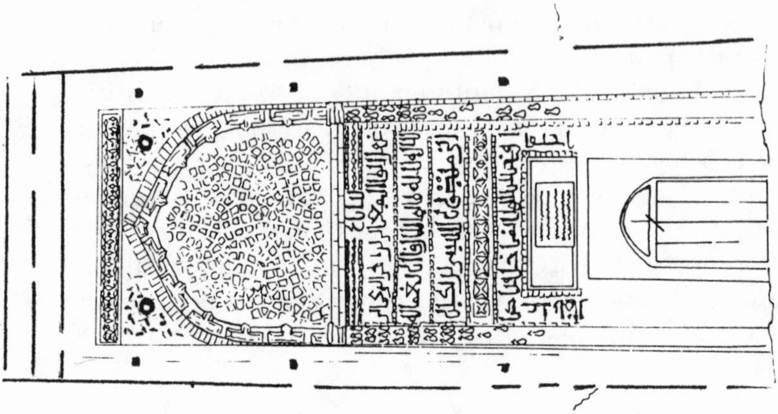

20. *Kharraqān II entrance, Kharraqān. Saljūq period. A.D. 1093-4. After a photo in Stronach and Young.*

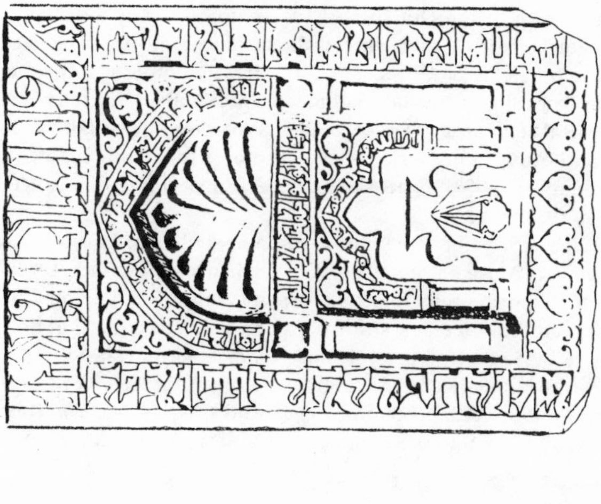

21. *Marble stone with mihrab design, Iran. Saljūq period. 12th. century A.D. After a photo in Féhervári (1972).*

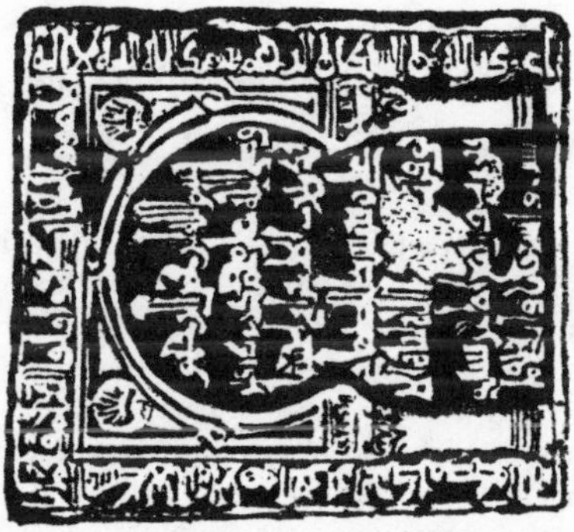

22. *Mihrab-shaped funerary stone, Cordoba. Almoravid period. A.D. 1103. After a photo in Smith, Bray and Ezzy.*

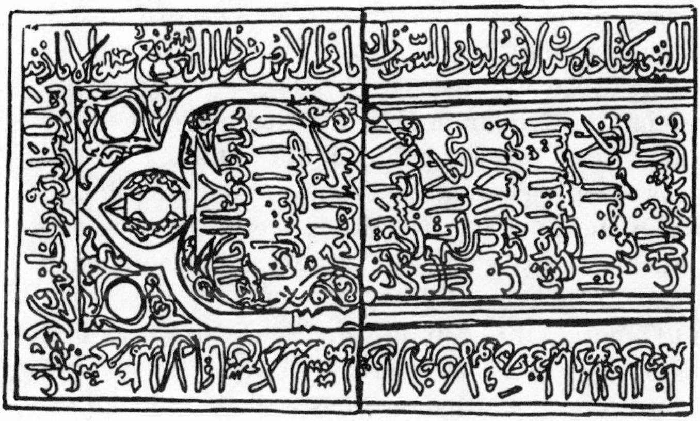

23. *Tombstone with mihrab design, Iran. Late Saljūq or early Il-Khānid period. 13th. century A.D. After a photo in* The David Collection.

the presence of miḥrāb's spandrel medallions on entrances,[71] Qur'ānic epigraphy and the fact that, so far as I can tell, these miḥrāb-like entrances are found on the religious rather than the secular structures.

If this relationship is intentional, then *a* meaning of the miḥrāb must have been sought for the entrance panels. Clearly, this meaning cannot be the use of the miḥrāb as a directional niche since very few of these entrances are oriented toward Mecca. We must thus seek other meanings of the miḥrāb.

I should mention that miḥrāb-like designs are also found on tombstones. In fact, the similarity between tombstones and miḥrābs is so great that at times a distinction is possible only on a epigraphic basis.[72] Here, too, it is clear that a meaning of the miḥrāb beyond its function as a directional niche was intended.

Although the etymology of the word *miḥrāb* is uncertain and its original function in early Islam not clear,[73] there is,

71. These spandrel medallions (sometimes appearing as semi-spherical knobs) are found on miḥrābs, tombstones, building records, arches, and entrance panels. The meaning of these medallions becomes better understood when we observe that in most cases the right medallion is inscribed with the name of Allah and the left bears the name of Muḥammad, clearly indicating the presence of Allah and Muḥammad as heavenly signs or light (planets). In fact, in some later examples such as the entrance portal of Masjid-i Jāmī of Naṭanz the medallions have sunburst patterns indicating their planetary symbolsim. The concept of God as light and Muḥammad as the light of God is a fundamental principle of Muslim faith. The term light of God occurs thirteen times in the Qur'ān and the Islamic sources are filled with the expressions of such symbolism (for the Islamic doctrines of light, see T.J. De Boer, *Encyclopedia of Islam,* s.v. *"Nūr"*). It will, however, suffice to quote a passage from al-Ghazālī's (Muḥammad b. Muḥammad Ghazali of Ṭūs, d. 505/1111), *Mishkāt al-Anwār:* "Praise to Allah! Who poureth forth light; and giveth sight; and from His mysterious height removes the veils of night! And prayer for Muḥammad! Of all lights the light;. . ." [Ed. and trans. by W.H.T. Gardner (Lahore, 1952), p. 75].

72. Géza Fehérvári, "Miḥrāb or Tombstone? A Speculation," in *Islamic Art in The Metropolitan Museum of Art,* ed. R. Ettinghausen (New York, 1972), p. 241.

73. For studies on the miḥrāb see Pederson's article in *Encyclopedia of Islam,* s.v. "Miḥrāb." An excellent study on its meaning as a place of honor in the palace is by Sauvaget in *La mosquée omeyyade,* pp. 145-149. Other useful articles are R.J. Sarjeant, "Miḥrāb," *Bulletin of the School of Oriental and African Studies,* XXII (1959), pp. 439-52 and Oleg Grabar, *The Formation of Islamic Art* (New Haven, 1973), pp. 120-2. Also see B.C. Miles, "Miḥrāb and

however, some evidence to suggest that in the earlier Islamic times the word *miḥrāb* signified, at least as one of its functions, a place of burial. Géza Fehérvári is one who gives some credence to such a theory. He cites from Ibn Rusta's *Kitāb al-A'lāq al-Nafisa* that in the Great Mosque of Sanā' in Yemen "There was a *qabr* of one of the prophets in the place of the miḥrāb." He also refers to Ibn Baṭṭūṭa's comment that "Three hundred prophets were buried in the qibla," as a possible clue to miḥrāb's funerary function in the earlier periods.[74] Yūsuf Rāghib, likewise, in his article "Les premiere monuments funéraires de l'Islam" gives more examples of burials behind miḥrābs in the early Islamic period.[75]

I suggest that this funerary meaning of the miḥrāb, also supported by its use on tombstones, may have been mostly related to its significance as a symbol of a rite of passage. Oleg Grabar has already suggested that the decoration and the shape of the miḥrāb at Cordova "appears as a sort of a door with the possible mystical connotation of the way in which the divine grace comes to the faithful."[76] A similar idea is proposed by Melikian-Chirvani who speculates on the symbolism of the miḥrāb as *"Bāb ol Ma'refat,* the door of knowledge leading into the celestial garden."[77]

An explanation accepted by Ernst Herzfeld is the definition of miḥrāb as the "place of lance" derived from the Arabic word *ḥarba,*[78] meaning to battle. A mystical interpretation of this definition found in the writings of the fourteenth century A.D. mystic Abūl-Mafākher Yaḥyā Bākharzī adds credence to the meaning of miḥrāb as a symbol of passage. He wrote in his book *Awrād al-Aḥbāb wa Fuṣūṣ al-Ādāb* that,

---

'Anāzah: A Study in Early Islamic Iconography," *Archaeologica Orientalia in Memoriam Ernst Herzfeld* (N.Y., 1952), pp. 1689.

74. *Kitāb al-A'lāq al-Nafisa,* ed. M.J. de Goeje (Leiden, 1892), p. 110; trans. by Gaston Wiet as *Les atours précieux* (Cairo, 1955), p. 123 and *"Miḥrāb or Tombstone?"* p. 252.

75. *Annales Islamologiques,* IX (1970), p. 35.

76. *Formation of Islamic Art,* p. 121.

77. "The Sufi Strain in the Art of Kashan," *Oriental Art,* 12/4 (1966), p. 254.

78. *Geschichte der Stadt Samarra* (Berlin, 1948), p. 202.

> Etymologically speaking these three letters *ḥā, rā,* and *bā* indicate battle, tools (of warfare) and place (of warfare), like *ḥarb, ḥarab,* miḥrāb, and *ḥarba.* In gnosis, that place where in your prayers and communications with God you become aware of Him, is called miḥrāb. For it (miḥrāb) is a place of battle, *fanā,* and the destruction of satans . . .[79]

Thus, the miḥrāb represents a spiritual direction by being a symbol of salvation and redemption through prayers and worship. This meaning is also amply brought out in the mystical writings of Farīd al-Dīn 'Aṭṭār who, among many others, views the miḥrāb as a gateway of ontological mutation.[80]

The entrances of the tomb structures, as well as entrances to mosques and madrasas, may therefore have signified a rite of passage because of their miḥrāb-like shapes. It is reasonable to conclude that if the miḥrāb design of the entrances was intentional, then these passageways indicated a baptismal-like rite wherein one would undergo a spiritual transition quite similar to that intended by the miḥrāb-like tombstones (figs. 22-23).[81]

The Dome

There is no doubt that the dome played an important symbolic role in funerary structures. The use of the term dome *(gunbad, qubba)* to signify the tomb structure is sufficient proof of its importance. Clearly, the choice of the term *gunbad* (dome) was intended to attribute to this class

79. Ed. I. Afshār (Tehrān, 1966), p. 247.
در اصل لغت این سه حرف ح، ر، ب را بر جنك وآلات ومكان او دلالت است. مثل حرب وحراب ومحراب وحربه، ودر عرف آن مكانی كه در وقت حضور ومناجات باحق به او متوجه گردی محراب گويند از آن جهت كه محل نزاع ومقاتله نفس وشيطان وروح ورحمان است.
80. See Bākharzī's *Awrād al-Aḥbāb* (p. 248) for his views on the miḥrāb and his commentary on Farīd al-Dīn-i 'Aṭṭār's poem. "If you come to the monastery with us, you shall seek a different miḥrāb."
81. Miḥrāb-like tombstones are abundant. However, for a few elaborate examples see I. Afshār, "Two Twelve Century Gravestones of Yazd," *Studia Iranica,* 2/2 (1973), pp. 203 ff.; Esin Atil, *Exhibition of 2500 Years of Persian Art* (Washington D.C., 1971), fig. 83 and Ernst Kühnel, *The Minor Arts of Islam* (Ithaca, 1971), fig. 204.

of buildings the widely accepted cosmological and political symbolism of the dome.[82]

The symbolism of the dome as a manifestation of the universal archetype is ancient and widespread.[83] In Islamic Iran the use of such terms as *Gunbad-i Āsimānī, Gunbad-i Khaḍrā* and *Gunbad-i Kabūd* demonstrates its heavenly function. To quote from Sa'dī (d. 687/1292):

Behold yon azure dome, the sapphire sky
Reared in unpillared might its canopy
The vast pavillion gemm'd with world of light
Whose circling glories boast a boundless flight.[84]

In Niẓāmī's (d. 590/1194) *Haft Paykar* the seven domes of Bahrām symbolize the seven planets.[85] At Quṣayr 'Amra, the dome is pierced at its base by four cardinal openings flooding the light onto its inner surface, on which are painted the signs of the zodiac, thus identifying this dome as a model of the heavenly one (fig. 27). Clearly, as Grabar has suggested, the astronomical paintings of 'Amra dome "Suggest a wider meaning to the construction than mere usefulness in a hot room."[86]

Most of the domes in Islamic architecture bear similar signs that point to their heavenly imagery. The domes of the mausolea of Sulṭān Sanjar at Merv (1157-1160), the mosque at Qurwa, the tomb of Bābā Qāsim at Iṣfahān and the many vaults of the Friday Mosque of Iṣfahān bear ribbings that create stellar plans (fig. 24-26).[87] In most of these structures, similar to Quṣayr 'Amra, light pours upon the inner

82. I shall discuss the political symbolism of the dome in the chapter on the "Socio-Political Significance of the Tomb Structure."
83. See E.B. Smith, *The Dome* (Princeton, 1951) for a detailed discussion of the symbolism of the dome among many different civilizations in the West.
84. Nader Ardelan and Lalaeh Bakhtiar, *The Sense of Unity* (Chicago, 1975), p. 136.
85. Ed. V. Dastgardī (Tehrān, 1936), pp. 145, 166, 186, 197, 216, 235, 267, 292.
86. "The Islamic Dome, Some Considerations," *Journal of the Society of Architectural Historians* (1963), p. 196, n. 24.
87. See Pope, *Survey*, VIII, plates 310, 303C, 309. Also see vol. III, figs. 464, 332-334. For Qurwa see Robert Hillenbrand, "Saljuq Monuments in Iran: I," *Oriental Art,* N.S. XVIII(1972), pp. 64-67 and Wolfram Kleiss, "Bericht über Erkundsfahrten in Iran im 1970," *Archaeologische Mitteilungen aus Iran,* N.F. 4(1971), pp. 100-104.

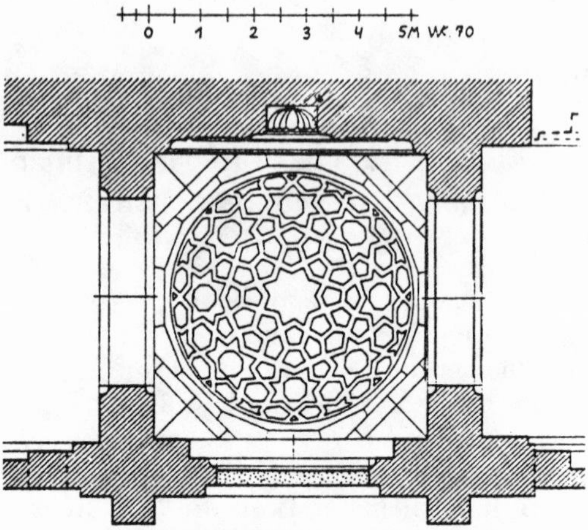

24. Interior surface of the dome of the mosque at Qurwa, Qurwa. Saljūq period. 12th. century. After Kleiss.

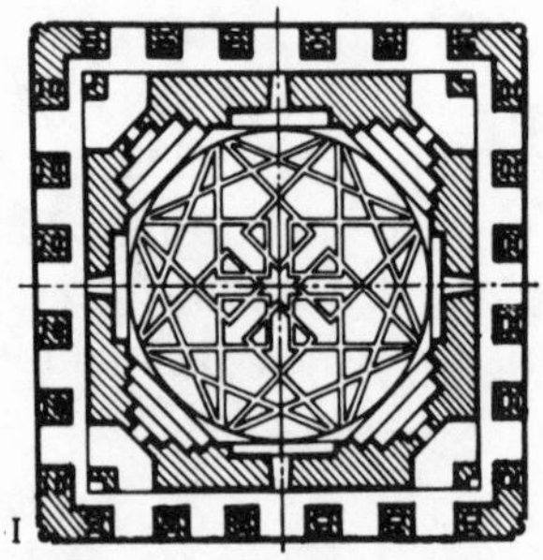

25. Interior surface of the dome of Sanjar's tomb, Merv. Saljūq period. A.D. 1157-60. After Brandenburg.

26. *Stellar vault of the Jāmi' Mosque, Isfahān. Saljūq period. 11th. century A.D. After Pope.*

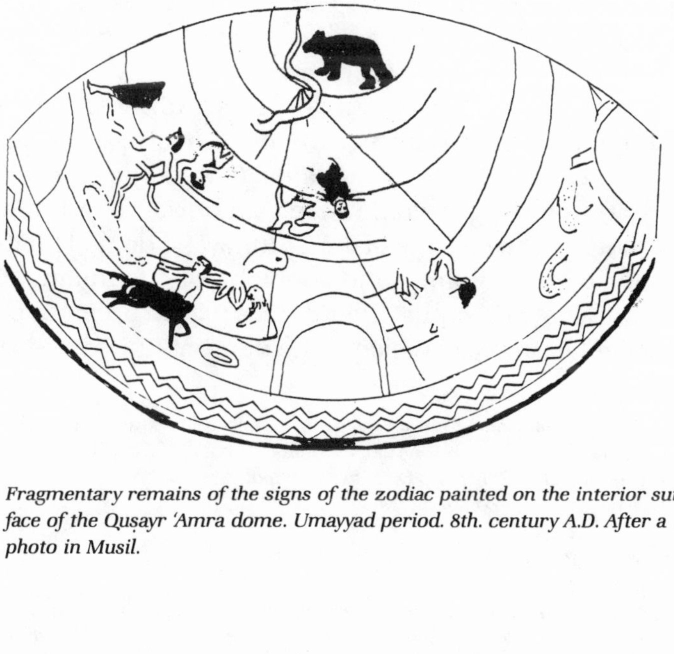

27. *Fragmentary remains of the signs of the zodiac painted on the interior surface of the Quṣayr 'Amra dome. Umayyad period. 8th. century A.D. After a photo in Musil.*

surface of the dome through base windows. Therefore, the heavenly aspects of the stellar designs are emphasized.[88] In Masjid-i Jāmī of Varāmīn (720-1/1325-6), the name Allāh is placed repeatedly in the ribbed star of its dome, which brings home the strongest message of the dome's heavenly symbolism (plate 18). The stalactite domes of the Spanish Nāṣirids and Almohāds give further impressive examples of canopies attempting to reflect the heavenly bodies (plate 19).

Vincenzo Strika has suggested that even the conical domes and especially the imbricated pine cone shaped ones used in the mausolea of Iraq and south-west Iran (plate 20) symbolize the tree of life and stand for resurrection and are thus imbued with heavenly-paradisaic significance.[89]

The paradisaic symbolism of the dome is also evident in the narrative quoted earlier from *Mujmal al-Tawārīkh wa'l Qiṣāṣ* where Ḥāmid, the hero of the story, discovers in his search for the source of the river Nile that the dome of the *chāhār-ṭāq* is "The Paradise."[90] Likewise in Qummī's account of a descendant of Imām Ja'far he uses the terms dome, shade and holy interchangeably, which indicated the dome's symbolism as a paradisaic element.[91]

Similar accounts pointing to the paradisaic symbolism of the dome (by associating the dome with water) can be found in Ibn al-Balkhī's *Fārs-nāma*. In it he speaks of a *chāhār-ṭāq* from whose dome water (an attribute of Paradise) flowed.[92] In the mosque of Ibn Ṭūlūn was a domed building resting on ten columns under which was a fountain.[93] One can speak of numerous other domes placed upon water, an excellent example of which is the dome at Khirbat al-Mafjar

88. On the symbolism of astral designs in Islamic architecture see V. Strika, "La Cathedra di S. Pietro A Venezia: Note Sulla Simbologia Astrale nell'Arte Islamica," *Annali dell' Instituto Orientale di Napoli*, 38/2 (1978).
89. "The Turbah of Zumurrud Khātūn," pp. 284ff.
90. See n. 51.
91. See n. 49.
92. See n. 51.
93. Maqrizī, *Khitāt* (Cairo, 1855), II:268-269, cited in Oleg Grabar, "The Islamic Dome, Some Considerations," *Journal of The Society of Architectural Historians* (1963), p. 195.

placed over a shallow pool.[94] The shallowness of the pool suggests a meaning more symbolically profound than that generally accepted as an expression of the Caliph's revelry.[95] The paradisaic significance of these domes becomes evident when one reads of the Paradise like rendition of even those canopies that arched over the bathhouses *(ḥammāms)* of medieval Iran. An example is the following poem by ʿAbd al-Razāq-i Iṣfahānī (d. 588/1192) on domed baths:

> You ask yourself what is that circular shape whose ceiling rivals the heavenly dome.
> Like an *iwān* arched over
> a pavilion over the (holy) fire.
> Its air is clear and its water pleasant,
> its ground is pure and its ceiling radiant with light.
> . . . .
> Its fire is envied by (the fire of) immortality.
> Its pool of water shames the reservoir of nectar in Paradise.[96]

The Paintings of Kharraqān I

The paintings of Kharraqān I play an essential role in the understanding of the tomb structure's heavenly-paradisaic symbolism. Perhaps such paintings were common in the funerary architecture of medieval Iran. This seems probable when we consider the advanced and accomplished execution of the Kharraqān paintings. For the time being, however, these paintings should be considered one of the singular major works in the history of Iran's architectural decoration. They represent not only an imaginative plane of artistic creation in funerary architecture but also aspects of

94. R.W. Hamilton, *Khirbat al-Mafjar* (Oxford, 1959), pp. 110ff.
95. Richard Ettinghausen, *From Byzantium To Sassanian Iran and the Islamic World* (Leiden, 1972), pp. 18ff. and Grabar, "The Islamic Dome," p. 196.
96. This poem is left to us in the anthology of *Munis al-Aḥrār fī Daqā'iq al-Ashʿār* compiled by Muḥammad ibn Badr al-Jājarmī (741/1341), ed. Mir Ṣāleḥ Ṭabībī, 2 vols. (Tehrān, 1337/1958), I:79.

چه گوئی چیست آن شکل مدور   که دارد خیمه با گردون برابر
چه ایوانی کشیده بر سر آب   چو خرگاهی زده بر روی آذر
هوایش روشن و آبش موافق   زمینش صافی و سقفش منور
.....
ز آتش رشک برده حیوان   ز حوضش شرم خورده حوض کوثر

Islamic philosophy and thought that are unveiled in the writings of sages, philosophers and poets.

Of great importance is the fact that these paintings give further strength and support to the theory of the tomb's symbolism as an image of Paradise.

Inside Kharraqān I, in the lower half of every wall, save the entrance, there is a segmented niche with a painting of a glass lamp hanging from its apex (fig. 28, plate 21). On a primary level of interpretation, according to the Qur'ān's surah of *al-Nūr*, this glass lamp is the symbol of God and is the light of God:

> Allah is the Light of the heavens and the earth. The similitude of His light is as a niche wherein is a lamp. The lamp is in a glass. The glass is, as it were, a shining star. (This lamp is) kindled from a blessed tree, an olive, neither of the East nor of the West, whose oil would almost glow forth (of itself) though no fire touched it. Light upon light! Allah guideth unto His light whom He will. And Allah speaketh to mankind in allegories, for Allah is Knower of all things. (24:35)

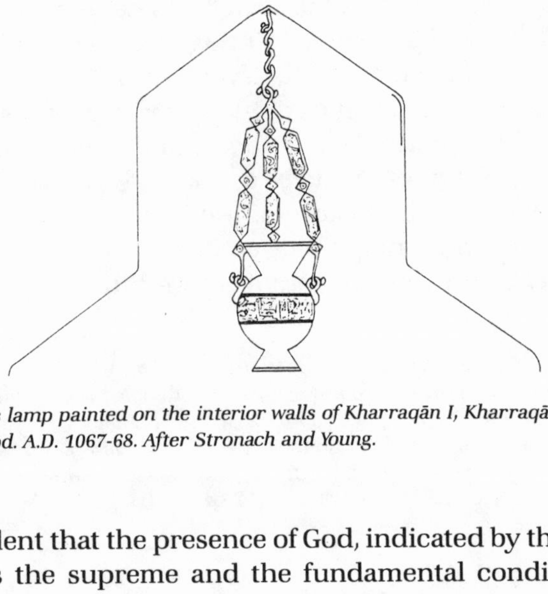

28. *Glass lamp painted on the interior walls of Kharraqān I, Kharraqān. Saljūq period. A.D. 1067-68. After Stronach and Young.*

It is evident that the presence of God, indicated by the glass lamp, is the supreme and the fundamental condition of

Paradise. To quote from the Qur'ān: "For the righteous are Gardens in nearness to their Lord . . ." (3:15). Moreover, we must carry our consideration one step further to the light emanating from the lamp. This divine light, for "Allah is the Light of the heavens and the earth," is apotropaic and protects the deceased from all evil. We find in the Qur'ān: ". . . And we adorned the lower heaven with lights, and (provided it) with guard . . ." (41:12).

In Niẓāmī's *Haft Paykar*, hell *(dūzakh)* is recognized by its heat and Paradise *(bihisht)* by its light.[97] To quote from the *Kashf al-Ḥaqāyiq* (c. 680/1272) of Sheikh 'Abd al-'Azīz ibn Muḥammad Nasafī:

> . . . The blessed being is the one who has emerged out of (the world of) temperament and darkness and has become luminous so as to join the ascending (height) that is the everlasting Paradise.[98]

However, a very interesting meaning of the glass lamp, relevant to funerary symbolism, is found in *The Kashf al-Maḥjūb* of al-Hujwīrī. He wrote:

> Abū Bakr Wāsitī has discoursed on the spirit more than any of the sufi shaykhs. It is related that he said, 'There are ten stations *(maqāmāt)* of spirits: (1) the spirits of the sincere *(mukhliṣīn)*, which are imprisoned in a darkness and know not what will befall them; . . . (4) the spirits of the beneficient *(ahl-i minān)*, which are hung in lamps of light from the throne of God, and their food is mercy, and their drink is favor and proximity; . . .[99]

In this quote, the lamp is symbolic of a paradisaic spirit, which makes its presence within a tomb quite fitting and

97. Ed. V. Dastgardī (Tehrān, 1936), p. 139.

98. Ed. 'A.M. Dāmghānī (Tehrān, 1966), p. 223.
We can of course mention endless sources speaking of light as a quality of Paradise. For the sake of clarity I shall give a few more examples relating light to the concepts of resurrection and Paradise. We read, for example, in Aḥmad Jām-i Zhende Pīl's *Miftāḥ al-Nijāt* (522/1128): "The Prophet, peace and blessings of God on him said to Abū Hurayra: teach my *sunna* to the people so that you will have light and be luminous on the day of resurrection!" Ed. 'A. Fāḍil (Tehrān: 1968), p. 60.

99. P. 265.

explains its presence on many tombstones (fig. 23). Moreover, as it has already been pointed out, this lamp is a sign of the fourth level of Paradise, a level intended as the resting place of the devout—a symbolism similar in function to the square domed structures with four openings. Thus the association of the tomb with the fourth level of Paradise is of universal significance and indicates strongly that this meaning is not accidental or unintended.

On every pier, in between the glass lamps, is the representation of a pomegranate tree with birds perched upon its branches (fig. 29). There are two birds on each side of the tree. This pomegranate tree too is expressive of the concept of Paradise since pomegranate is a fruit of Paradise (Qur'ān 55:68). As a result, the pomegranate tree has always been associated with perpetuity and life everlasting. According to Ibn al-Jauzi:

> The tree stands for enlightenment, the fruit relieves from hunger and thirst.[100]

The birds perched upon the branches of the pomegranate tree may indicate such paradisial qualities as audition and the Garden. One description of Paradise found in *Ṭarīq ut-Taḥqīq* of Sanā'ī is as follows:

> The city of our dwelling has for its floor the heavenly vault
> Its earth has the smell of anbar (and) the waters within it taste like sugar
> ....
> You will see parrots in this Garden, all their singing is the mention of the Lord (from Qur'ān 40:29)
> ....
> In meadows the nightingale will sing: our Lord is the most high. (from Qur'ān 87:1)[101]

A more appropriate description of Paradise is found in al-Hujwīrī's *The Kashf al-Mahjūb:*

100. Abu'l-Faraj ibn al-Jauzi, *Tablīs al-Iblīs,* ed. M. Munīr (Cairo, 1948), p. 385; partial translation by D.S. Margoliouth as "The Devils Delusion" in *Islamic Culture,* XII/3 (1938), p. 359. Also see P. Ackerman, *Survey,* I:856 for further reference to the pomegranate tree's sacred qualities.
101. Ed. and partially trans. by Bo Utas, Scandanavian Institute of Asian Studies, no. 13 (Lund, 1973), p. 9.

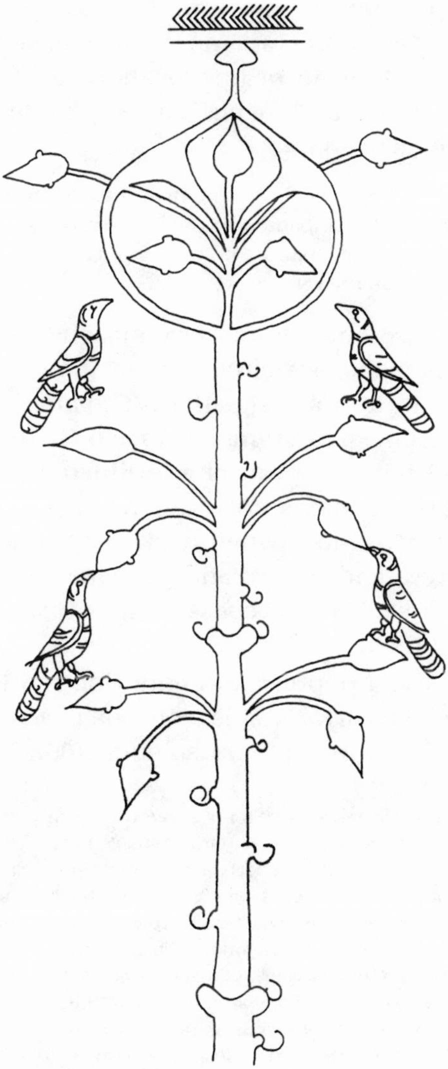

29. Pomegranate tree with birds painted on the interior piers of Kharraqān I, Kharraqān. Saljūq period. A.D. 1067-8. After Stronach and Young.

> It is stated in well known traditions that the inhabitants of Paradise enjoy audition, for there comes from every tree a different voice and melody.[102]

The birds perched in rows upon the branches of the trees also bring to mind Qur'ānic verses concerning Paradise and resurrection. According to surah 56, verse 22, Paradise is a place with "flesh of birds as may be desired" and in surah 24, verses 41-43:

> Seest thou not that all who are in the heavens and the earth celebrate the praises of Allah, and also the birds in rows upon rows . . . To Allah belongs the kingdom of the heavens and of the earth, and to Allah shall be the return.

Above the representation of every mosque lamp, within the arch of the niche, is a circular medallion with a pearl border, framed by a sunburst pattern. The interior space of each medallion encloses a symbolic image. On the entrance wall (side one) stands a peacock in full fan. On sides two and eight, the medallions enclose two rotating triangles. Two peacocks with intertwined necks are found on sides three and seven, and two rotating squares are found on sides four and six. Two peacocks confront each other on side five (fig. 30).

The peacock is a popular and enduring representation in medieval Islamic art.[103] Aside from the peacocks on the inside walls of Kharraqān I mausoleum (1067-68) painted

102. P. 399. Apparently the representation of a tree with birds perched upon its branches was a meaningful and important image in the arts of medieval Islam. Waṣṣāf (*Tarikh,* p. 352) reports a man-made paradisaic tree in the palace of Oljeitu whose branches were covered with jewels and birds. The poet al-Mutanabbī saw a tent which had a tree with birds painted upon it and was impressed enough to mention it in his poetry (J. Horowitz, "Die Leschreibung eines Gemaldes bei Mutanabbi," *Der Islam,* I (1910, 385-8). This last reference was brought to my attention by R. Hillenbrand (see "Tomb Towers of Iran to 1550," II:279). On the importance of the tree with birds also see A.J. Wensinck, "Tree and Bird as Cosmological Symbols in Western Asia," *Verhandelingen Der Koninklijke Akademie Van Wetenschappen Te Amsterdam,* (1921), p. 38.
103. For a study of the symbolism of the peacock see my article, "A Preliminary Study on the Iconography of the Peacock in Medieval Islam," in *The Proceedings of the University of Edinburgh Conference on Saljūq Art,* ed. by R. Hillenbrand, forthcoming.

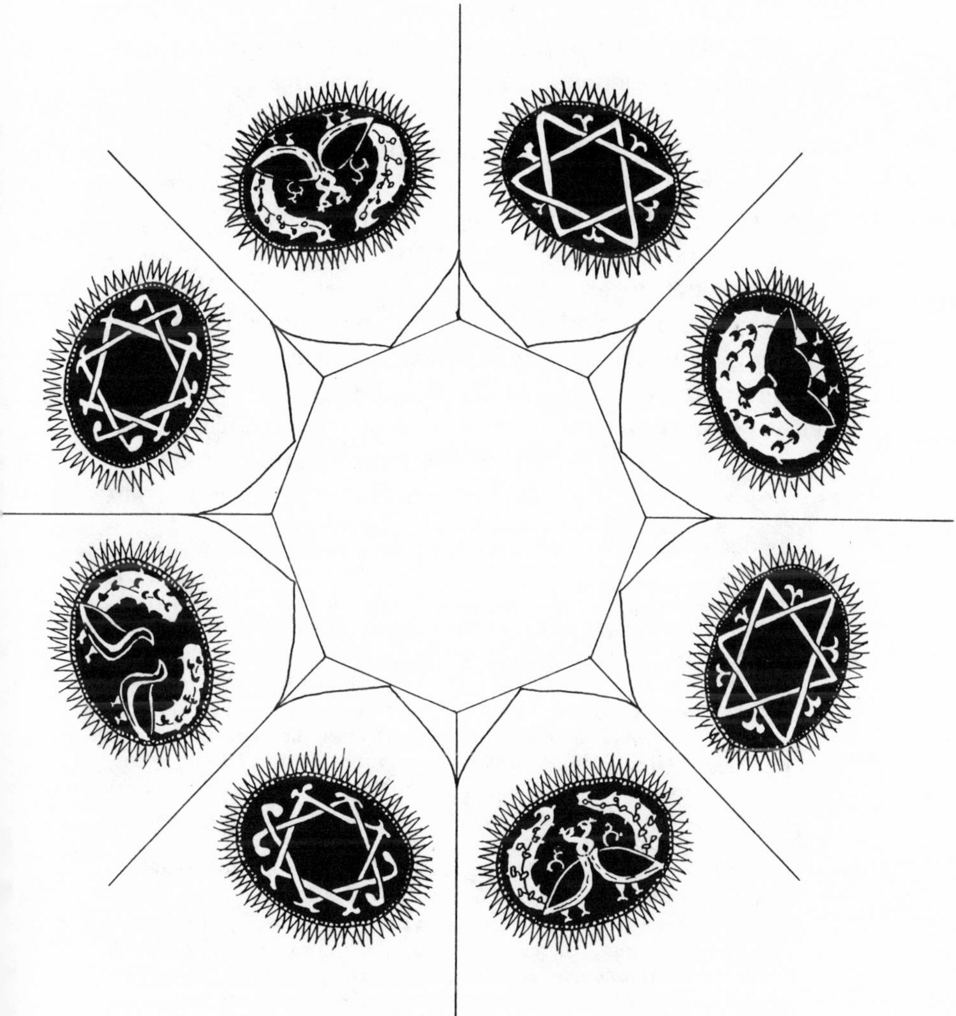

30. The scheme of the sunburst medallions painted on the interior walls of Kharraqān I, Kharraqān. Saljūq period. A.D. 1067-8. After Stronach and Young.

in full fan or with necks intertwined, peacocks also appear on early Islamic textiles either flanking the tree of life or in a confronting position (fig. 31).[104] The many other representations of peacocks sculpted in metal (fig. 32), painted on ceramics (fig. 33) and carved and engraved (fig. 34) raise innumerable questions concerning the meaning of this bird and its function in the early and middle ages of Islam.

Moreover its popularity in the Sassanian period (with the peacock's tail also appearing as the tail of the Senmurw) ensures us of the continuity of its significance over the span of a few centuries and across historical-cultural lines.[105]

To commence our study of peacock's iconography, I must first mention that the peacock despite its enormous popularity was also imbued with certain negative attributes. It was seen as a source of ill-omened events and its ugly feet and voice came to symbolize the darker side of the human

104. For early Būyid and Saljūq examples see: Eugene I Holt, "A Thousand Year Old Peacock," *Bulletin of the Los Angeles County Museum of Art*, 16/2 (1964), p. 11-4, fig. 1-2; Phyllis Ackerman, "Textile Designs in Andarz Nama," *A Survey of Persian Art*, XIII-Fascicle (1968), figs. 11, and 18, also *Survey*, XI, fig. 186B. Dorothy G. Shepherd, "Technical Aspects of the Būyid Silks," *Survey*, XIV, fig. 1507. For Spanish examples see Ralph Pinder Wilson, *Islamic Art* (N.Y., 1957), plate 62 also reproduced among others in David T. Rice, *Islamic Art* (N.Y., 1969), fig. 157. For a Mesopotamian example see G. Fehérvári, "Two Early 'Abbāsid Lustre Bowls," *Oriental Art*, IX/2 (1963), fig. 7. and Gaston Wiet's *Soieries Persanes* (Cairo, 1947) includes some interesting examples shown in plates IV, VII, XII, and XVIII.
For an example of a Sāmānid Buffware with peacocks placed around the figure of a cavalier, see *The David's Collection of Islamic Art* (Copenhagen, 1975), plate 22. Also *ibid.*, plates 61-62 for representations of peacocks on a mina'i ware. For more examples of peacocks on mina'i see Pope, *Survey*, X, plate 657B. For representations of peacocks on an Ayyūbid ceramic ware see Abū-l-Faraj al-Ush, *Musée National de Damas* (Damascus, 1976), plate XV. For a few examples of peacocks painted on Saljūq lustre ware see *Survey*, X, figs. 935A, and 641A. For some examples of peacocks as metal sculpture see Carel J. Dury, *Art of Islam* (N.Y., 1970), plate on p. 81. Also *Islamic Art Across the World, An Exhibition at Indiana University Art Museum* (Bloomington, 1970), plate 69.

105. According to Hanns-Peter Schmidt the peacock does not play a prominent iconographic role in Sassanian art. This may have been partly due to the popularity of the Senmurw which had borrowed the peacock's tail and had thus rendered the representation of the bird in its entirety useless. See "Senmurw" in *Persica*, IX (1980), p. 45.

31. Peacocks with feline prey, Rayy. Būyid period. 10th. century A.D. After Wiet.

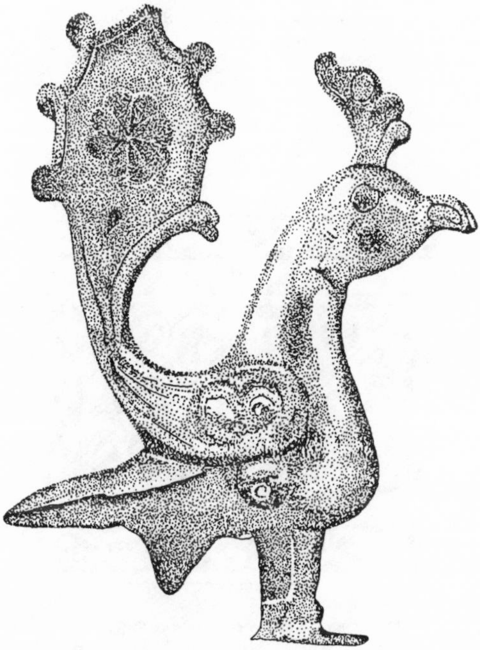

32. A bronze peacock, Iran. Saljūq period. 12th. century A.D. After DuRy.

33. *Figure of a peacock from a lustre vase, Iraq or Iran. 'Abbāsid period. 10th. century A.D. After a photo in Dimand.*

34. *Peacock carved in wood, Egypt. Fatimid period. 11th. century A.D. After Jenkins (1972).*

soul. The Saljūq poet Niẓāmī, for example, warns us against attraction to outward appearances and asks that we should not judge a cat or a peacock by their beautiful looks but by their ugly cries—the cry being a reference to the soul. He wrote:

> Do not judge a peacock by the color of its feathers and the manner of its flight, for like the cat he too has an ugly cry.[106]

Likewise, in reference to the ugliness of its feet which symbolizes the world, versus its tail that stands for the heavens, the mystic poet Ḥakīm Sanā'ī (d. 548/1152) wrote:

> If the peacock's feet were like its feathers, it would shine splendid by day and night.[107]

The negative symbolism of the peacock is brought across quite effectively when Kamāl al-Dīn Muḥammad ibn Mūsā al-Damīrī (d. 808/1405) quotes a man named *Ṭāwūs* (Peacock) describing himself in self-deprecating terms:

> I am 'Abd al-Na'īm
> I am the Peacock of hell
> I am more ill-omened than anything
> that walks upon this earth.[108]

Similarily Abī 'Uthmān 'Amr ibn Baḥr al-Jāḥiẓ (d. 254/868) speaks of the superstitions and pessimistic views of the Arabs toward the peacock when he writes:

> It is claimed by Ja'far ibn Sa'īd that the rooster is praiseworthier than the peacock. . . . The rooster is free from the ugliness of the

106. *Sharaf-nāma*, ed. V. Dastgardī (Tehrān, 1936), p. 256.

مبین رنك طاووس وپرواز او   که چو گربه زشت آمد آواز او

107. *Ḥadīqatu'L-Ḥaqīqat*, ed. and translated by Major J. Stephenson (N.Y., 1972), p. 37; Persian text p. 24.

پای طاووس اگر چه پر بودی   بشب و روز جلوه کر بودی

108. *Ḥayāt al-Ḥayawān al-Kubrā*, 2 vols. (Cairo, n.d.), I:654.

إننى عبد النعيم   أنا طاووس الجحيم
وانا اشام من يمشي   على ظهر الحطيم

Also see on the same page such sayings as "more ill-omened than the peacock," etc.

> peacock and from the stupidity and ugliness of its face, and from the pessimism of the inhabitants of the house toward him and the ugliness of its leg and its vile appearance.[109]

The root of this negativity toward the peacock rests in the belief that the peacock seduced Adam and Eve into eating the forbidden grain and was thus the cause of their, as well as his own, expulsion from the Garden of Paradise. References to this episode are abundant in the medieval literature of Islam. For brevity's sake I cite only from Afḍal al-Dīn Khāqānī (d. 595/1199) and Bardsīrī Kirmānī. The former wrote in recognition of the fall of peacock from Paradise that: "(Alas) the tail of the peacock of Paradise is now viewed as a fan to ward off flies."[110] And to quote again from Khāqānī we readily recognize the disgraceful position of the peacock in such phrases as: "Like that peacock who leads the Satan by day and night."[111]

Bardsīrī identifies the peacock of Paradise as an allegory for the sexual desires of Eve which forced Adam to succumb to the black snake who is one manifestation of Satan.[112] Illustrative references to this theme can be found, for example, in a copy of 'Aṭṭār's (d. 589/1193) *Manṭiq al-Ṭayr* of 1483 where a peacock is lamenting over his fall from grace.[113] Another example can be seen in an Ottoman miniature illustrating the Persian manuscript of 'Alā al-Dīn Manṣūr's "Lives of the Prophets and of the Four Orthodox Caliphs."

109. *Kitāb al-Ḥayawān*, ed. 'A.M. Hārūn, 8 vols. (Cairo, 1949), 2:243-244.

وكان جعفر بن سعيد، يزعم أنّ الدّيك أحمدُ من الطاووس ... إذا مشى، سليم من مقابح (ومن موقه وقبح صورته) ومن تشاؤم اهل الدار (به، و) من قبح رجليه ونذالته مرآته.

110. Cited in Z. Khānlarī, *Rāhnamāy-i Adabīyāt-i Fārsī* (Tehrān, 1962), p. 250.

دم طاووس بهشتی را مگس ران بین

111. *Dīvān*, ed. 'A. Rassūlī (Tehrān, 1971), p. 658.

رهبر دیو چو طاووس مدام

112. *Miṣbāh al-Arwāḥ*, ed. B. Furūzānfar (Tehrān, 1970), pp. 26-27.

طاووس چه بود حسن هوا ابلیس هوی ومار سودا

113. See fig. 5 in Marie Lukens Swietochowski, "The Historical Background and Illustrative Character of the Metropolitan Museum's 'Manṭiq al-Ṭayr' of 1483," ed. R. Ettinghausen, Islamic Art in the Metropolitan Museum of Art (N.Y., 1972). .

Here a peacock in full fan stands next to a snake and the Biblical couple while an angel watches them all.[114]

This so-called dark episode in the life of the peacock is clearly the source of Yazīdids belief in *Malik Ṭāwūs,* the peacock-angel who in their case, ultimately repents and by that he once again leads his followers into the Paradise.[115]

Despite all this adverse publicity it is interesting to note that the peacock has always managed to attract rather than repel the imagination of the Muslims and regardless of its reprobating role in the fall of Adam and Eve this bird was viewed almost perenially as an indispensible feature of Paradise. There are not too many sources which do not identify the peacock with Paradise or vice-versa. Al-Jāḥiẓ, for example, names the peacock as an occupant of Paradise.[116] In Jalāl al-Din Rūmī's (d. 672/1273) poetry the higher house of Paradise is adorned by a peacock whose name is *"Ṭāwūs Illyīn."*[117] Similarly, the poet Shams Ṭabasī (d. 626/1227) speaks of *"Ṭāwūs Sadrat al-Muntahā"* which is the peacock of the uppermost level of Paradise.[118] Furthermore, there are indeed few descriptions of Paradise or paradise-like gardens that do not include the peacock. Muffaḍḍal ibn Sa'd al-Māfarrukhī's *Maḥāsin Iṣfahān* (written 421/1030) describes the paradisaic gardens of Aḥmad Sīāh and Bikr in Iṣfahān as places where the peacock was one of its eminent features.[119] Likewise in Abūl-Naṣr al-'Utbī's (d. 427/1035) *Tārīkh Yamīnī* references to beautiful and paradisaic landscapes cannot be devoid of peacocks.[120]

114. See fig. 9 in Emil Esin, *Mecca and Medina* (N.Y., 1963).
115. T. Menzel, "Yazīdī," *Encyclopedia of Islam.*
116. *Kitāb al-Ḥayawān,* 3:395.
117. Ed. and trans. by R.A. Nicholson, 3 vols., E.J.W. Gibb Memorial (London, 1977), p. 42.
118. *Dīvān,* ed. T. Bīnish (Mashad, 1964), p. 8.
119. *Tarjuma-yi Maḥāsin-i Iṣfahān* (tr. into Persian by al-Riḍā Āwī in A.H. 729 from Māfarrūkhī's Arabic text 421/1031), (Tehrān, 1949), pp. 27-28.
120. Cited in *Tarjuma-yi Tārīkh-i Yamīnī,* which is a translation of 'Utbī's Arabic *Tārīkh-i Yamīnī* into Persian by the 8th./14th. century writer Nāṣiḥ ibn Ẓafar al-Jurfādqānī. Edited by J. Shu'ār (Tehrān, 1966), p. 25.

These gardens, clearly the properties of the nobility and the aristocracy, were almost always adorned with peacocks. The peacock helped to render these landscapes as earthly models of the heavenly Paradise. The proof of this is put forth by a variety of sources. The Saljūq historian al-Rāwandī (b. circa 550's/1160's) describes the garden of Qīlich Arslān in all of its splendor as follows:

> There were in his beloved garden of penetrating splendor;
> the nightingale, the parrot and the peacock.[121]

And the poet Azraqī Harawī (d. 526/1132) speaks of the paradise-like garden of Sulṭān Tughānshāh as a place where the great abundance of the feathers from the tail of the peacock and the body of the parrot had become the foundation block of every nest and the ground cover of pasturelands. He wrote:

> From the tail of the peacock and the feather of the parrot; the deer's verdant meadow and the nightingale's nests are made.[122]

The Saljūq poet Jamāl al-Dīn Iṣfahānī (d. 588/1192) wrote in a panegeric to the Saljūq minister Qawām al-Dīn:

> (In your garden) the earth is the color of the crown of the Indian parrot; the branches are fanned like the tail of the peacock of Paradise.[123]

It is thus obvious that the peacock was not only a feature of the royal paradisaic gardens but a symbol of it as well. Examples of this are also abundantly portrayed in the artifacts of medieval Islam where cavaliers and noblemen are shown in landscapes adorned and inhabited by peacocks (figs. 35,36).

121. *Rāḥatu's-Ṣudūr,* p. 459.

باد درباغ مرداش جلوه گر　　　　عندليب وطوطى وطاووس نر

122. Cited in Riḍā Qulī Khān-i Hidāyat's, *Mujma' al-Fuṣaḥā,* 6 vols. ed. M. Muṣṣaffā (Tehrān, 1957), 1:377.

از پر طوطى ودم طاووس كرده اند　　　　آهو وعندليب چراگاه وآشيان

123. *Ibid.,* 1:483.

خاك چو طوطى هندوستان سر اندر نهاد
شاخ چو طاووس فردوس پراندر پر زده است

35. *Cavalier in a landscape inhabited by peacocks. Buffware bowl, Nishāpūr. Sāmānid period. 10th. century A.D. After a photo in* The David Collection.

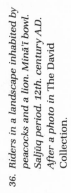

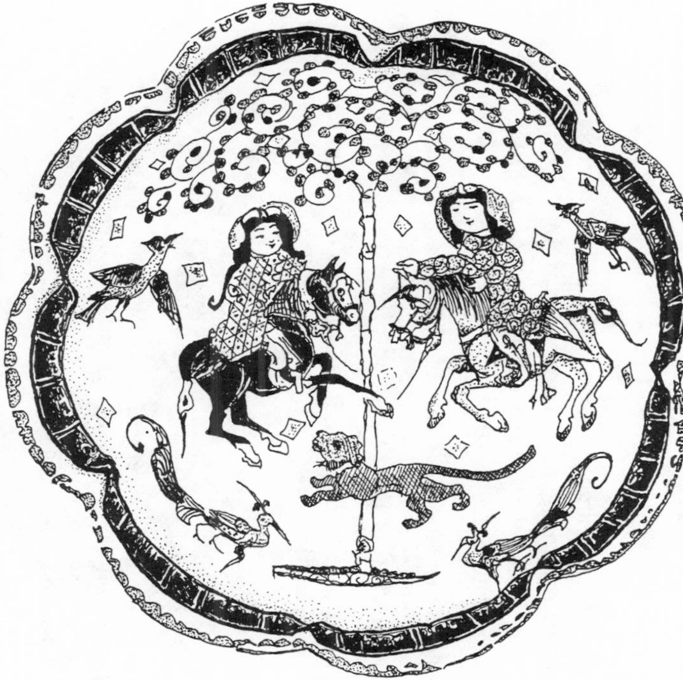

36. *Riders in a landscape inhabited by peacocks and a lion. Minā'ī bowl. Saljūq period. 12th. century A.D. After a photo in* The David Collection.

The peacock's association with Paradise was further reinforced by its meaning as a source of water, abundance, fertility and ultimately the season of spring. The poet Manūchihrī Dāmghānī (d. 432/1040) wrote:

> Winter died and spring came like a peacock.[124]

And on the arrival of the fall season he wrote:

> (Fall) cut away the tail of the peacock of spring and cast its feathers aside to a corner.[125]

In 'Aṭṭār's poetry the peacock is an exhalted and divine being to whom drought-stricken men plead for the end of the drought. He wrote in his *Illāhī-nāma:*

> One year a famine appeared and the people suffered great hardship. A crowd of people, bewildered and desperate, approached *Ṭā'ūs* in their desire for rain, saying: "There is no sign of rain, pray to God that he may grant it for us."[126]

The peacock because of its tail being adorned with eyes also became associated with a number of heavenly bodies. The most notable and the strongest of these associations is with the sun. The planetary association of peacock with the sun, itself a symbol of the fourth level of Paradise, strengthened the peacock's heavenly-paradisaic significance. Niẓāmī is especially fond of using the imagery of the peacock's fanned tail for the sun. He wrote:

> As the peacock sun took flight the *lājwardī* sky turned into gold.[127]

And:

> The peacock whose feathers are the sun, does not deserve admonishment for its feet.[128]

124. *Dīvān,* ed. D. Sīāqī (Tehrān, 1977), p. 127.

رفت سرما وبهار آمد چو طاووس

125. *Ibid.,* p. 147.

طاووس بهاری را دنبال بکندند پرش ببریدند و بکنجی بفکندند

126. Persian text ed by F. Rūḥānī (Tehrān, 1972), p. 162. English translation from J.A. Boyle's Illāhī-nāma (Manchester, 1976), p. 191.
127. *Iqbāl-nāma,* ed. V. Dastgardī (Tehrān, 1936), p. 190.

جو طاووس خورشید بگشاد بال زر اندود شد لاجوری هلال

128. *Makhzan al-Asrār,* ed. V. Dastgardī (Tehrān, 1936), p. 41.

در پر طاووس که زر پیکرست سرزنش پای کجا در خورست

The Saljūq poet Shams-i Ṭabasī (d. 624/1227) wrote:

> On this tourquoise colored canopy is a peacock of golden feathers.[129]

The mystic poet ʿAṭṭār refers to the peacock as the bride of this green canopy,[130] and wrote in his *Khusrau-nāma:*

> When this golden peacock began its journey the world was transformed into gold.[131]

A common name for the sun in medieval Persian literature is *ṭāwūs atish parr* (peacock with the wings of fire). To quote from Khāqānī:

> See the peacock with wings of fire in the azure heavens, from whose fanning the world has turned into a golden ornament.[132]

And for Rūdakī (d. 329/940) the peacock is a metaphor for the sun in its east-west journey. He wrote:

> It rises from Khurāsān like a peacock and rushes to the west triumphantly.[133]

Depictions of peacocks as a symbol of the sun are quite common. This identification is in most cases quite easy due to the presence of a sun disk, as identified convincingly by Géza Fehérvári, on the bird's body.[134] To cite a few examples from this genre: a bronze sculpture of a peacock which appropriately enough bears a sun disk upon its tail (fig. 32) and a peacock on an ʿAbbāsid lustre vase bearing a sun disk on its body (fig. 33).[135]

129 *Dīvān,* ed. T. Bīnish (Mashad, 1964), p. 48.

برین سقف زمرد فام طاووسیت زرین پر

130. *Khusrau-nāma,* ed. ʿA. Khunsārī (Tehrān, 1976), p. 236.

131. *Ibid.,* p. 236.

چو این طاووس زرین در حمل شد زمانه بازر رکن بدل شد

132. *Dīvān,* ed. ʿA. ʿAbd al-Rasūlī (Tehrān, 1978), p. 188.

در آبگون قفس بین طاووس آتشین پر کز پر گشادن او آفاق بست زیور

133. *Farhang-i Dihkhudā,* i.v. "*Ṭāwūs.*"

از خراسان بر دمد طاووس فش سوی خاور می شتابد شادو کش

134. Géza Fehérvári, "Two Early ʿAbbāsid Lustre Bowls," *Oriental Art,* IX/2 (1969), pp. 79-84.

135. For further examples see *Ibid.,* fig. 7 where a 10th century Mesopotamian silk bears the image of a peacock with a solar disk. Also Meyer-Riefstahl, *The Parrish Watson Collection of Muhammadan Potteries* (Paris, 1922), fig. 37. For similar themes on mina'i ceramics see *Ibid.,* note 38.

The solar symbolization of the peacock is also present in its representations within the funerary context as a bird of Paradise. At Kharraqān I, for example (fig. 30), the peacocks are enclosed within disks of radiating light that bespeak their astral or solar significance. Likewise, the peacocks shown flanking the tree of life on the Būyid funerary textile indicate a similar solar-astral iconography (fig. 31). Arthur Pope wrote of these birds:

> Peacocks carrying on their tails the starred lustre of the midnight sky in the lozenge frame of the ancient moon symbol . . . signaling their preeminence by clutching solar feline as prey.[136]

Pope was right, regardless of not presenting any concrete evidence for his assumption, for the felines on this textile are marked by solar disks that imbue the entire scene with astral significance.

The merging of the solar and paradisaic ideas is of course quite appropriate. For light is a quality of Paradise and an identifying sign of God. Above all, as I have already mentioned, the peacock's symbolization of the sun can also be viewed as an allusion to the fourth level of Paradise.

At times the peacock's tail is also associated with other astral bodies such as the moon, Mercury, and Jupiter.

Manūchihrī Dāmghānī likens the tail of the peacock to the moon. To quote a few verses from his *Dīvān*, he wrote:

> The moon has risen from the tail of the peacock.[137]

And,

> There is in any peacock's tail one hundred moons and thirty moons.[138]

136. Arthur U. Pope, *Masterpieces of Persian Art,* (N.Y., 1945), p. 72 and Gaston Wiet, *Soieries Persanes* (Cairo, 1947), p. 48.

137. *Dīvān,* p. 180.

از دم طاووس نر ماهی سر بر زده است

138. *Ibid.,* p. 60.

بر دم هر طاووس صدقمروسی قمر

Or,

> (As) The moon is on the tail of the peacock, the crown is on the head of the hoopoe.[139]

The peacock's association with Jupiter is attested in al-Bīrūnī's *al-Tafhīm* (written A.D. 1027) wherein the peacock is one of the indications of this lucky and paradisaic planet.[140] In Shams al-Dīn-i Ayyūb Dunīsary's *Navādir al-Tabādur li-Tuhfat al-Bahādur* (written 669/1271) the peacock is an indication of Mercury, the planet of writers and thinkers.[141]

The peacock therefore is a paradisaic bird. This particular meaning is further reinforced by its significance as a symbol of fertility, season of spring and the planet sun. Its presence within the tomb is on a very simple level an indication of the tomb's heavenly-paradisaic significance and points to the ultimate destination for the deceased. Thus its depiction on funerary textiles and in tombs is inevitably linked with the concept of life everlasting.[142]

The question now is whether or not the four remaining images within the medallions also have planetary significance. I believe that they do, and I have, therefore, put forth two explanations in the hope of stimulating further research on this subject. I personally favor the first explanation, although it is quite possible that its designers may have intended to convey both of these meanings since they are complementary.

139. *Ibid.*, p. 59.

بر دم طاووس ماه بر سر هدهد کلاه

140. Translated by Ramsey Wright as *The Book of Instruction in the Elements of the Art Astrology* (London, 1934), p. 247.

141. Ed. I. Afshār and M. T. Dānishpazhūh (Tehrān, 1971), p. 53. See also Eva Baer, *Sphinxes and Harpies* (Jerusalem, 1965), p. 73.

142. Öney in an article on the Kharraqān I frescoes relates the peacocks to the concept of Paradise due to the presence of pomegranates, a fruit of Paradise, on the walls of the mausoleum. But as we have seen the peacock can be indicative of Paradise without the pomegranate. See G. Öney, "The Interpretation of the Frescoes in the I. Kharragan Mausoleum Near Qazwin," *Akten des VII Internationalen Kongresses für Iranische Kunst und Archaologie, München, 1976* (Berlin, 1979), p. 403.

We may assume that the medallions (sides one to five clockwise or counterclockwise) represent the scheme of motion among planetary bodies. In other words, we may expect these drawings to represent an astronomical-astrological model of the heavens. As an explanation, here is a quote from Abu'l Rayḥān Muḥammad ibn Aḥmad al-Bīrūnī's *Kitāb al-Tafhīm li-Avā'il Ṣinā'at al-Tanjīm* (420/1029) which refers to the formation of aspects between planets:

> Whenever two planets are in signs which are in aspect to each other, they are also said to be in aspect; if they are in the same sign they are described as conjunct *(mujtama'īn),* while if they are at the same degree the conjunction is said to be partile *(muqtarīn).* If one of them is in a sign third from the other, they are in sextile aspect to the right or left; if in a fourth sign, to be in quartile; if in a fifth, in trine; and if in seventh, opposite. Should their degrees be equal they are called *muttaṣilīn,* for then between these aspects it is possible to construct either a regular hexagon, or a square or a triangle in the zodiac, or to divide it into two.[143]

Furthermore, the frequency of the occurence of these formations or aspects is limited to two trines, two sextiles, two quartiles, one conjunction and one opposition.[144]

These descriptions of the planetary aspects seem to bear similarity to the medallion representations at Kharraqān I. We can equate the two rotating triangles to the two trines, the two rotating squares to the two quartiles and the two opposing peacocks or peafowls to the opposition of the planets. The peacocks with intertwined necks can thus be considered to be the conjunction of the planets.[145] Now

143. *Elements of the Art of Astrology,* pp. 259-60.

144. *Ibid.,* p. 303.
The rotating trines and quartiles are a common motif in medieval Islamic art. Mostly they adorn the interior surfaces of vaults and domes as an indication of astral bodies. One should also mention, perhaps as a further reference to their astronomical-astrological meaning the rotating trines and squares on the western gates of the circular city of Heraqleh dating from circa tenth century. See Qasim Touir, "The First and Second Seasons at Heraqleh: 1976-1977," *Al-Arabiya al-Suriya,* 27-28 (1977-8), pp. 111-130.

145. Representations of peacocks with intertwined necks are found on Spanish Umayyad ivory carvings [see John Beckwith, *Caskets From Cordoba* (London, 1960), pp. 65, 68, and 69]; on the Pila of Jativa [see Eva Baer, "The Pila of Jativa: A Document of Secular Urban Art in Western Islam," *Kunst des Orients,* VII /2 (1970-71), pp. 151-152], on a Kobadabad tile [see Katharina Otto-Dorn,

this conjunction may well be the *muttaṣilīn,* while the peacock in full fan represents the *mujtama'īn* (conjunction in reality) of the planets. What is lacking in this system is the sextile aspect, but we can argue that the designers were not obsessed with a very accurate rendition of the planetary aspects, and the two pairs of trines also represent the sextile aspects.

37. Tile showing peacocks enclosed in rotating squares, Ghazna. Ghaznavid period. 11th. century A.D. After a photo in Jenkins(1983).

A red square Ghaznavid tile from Ghazni (fig. 37) displays a scheme which appears to be a variation of the Kharraqān system of medallions. Here two confronting peacocks are

---

"Bericht über die Grabung in Kobadabad 1966," *Archäologischer Anzeiger,* Heft 4 (1969), Taf. 1a], on an eleventh century penbox made by the Arabs in south Italy [see Ernst Kühnel, "Die Sarazenischen Olifanthorner" *Ib Berlin Museum* (1959), fig. 19] and on the interior paintings of Kharraqān I. It is also found in Armenian art, an example of which is illustrated in Eva Baer's *Sphinxes and Harpies,* plate XXXIV.

Eva Baer, in her article on the "Pila of Játiva," (p. 152) considers the intertwined peacocks to be purely decorative. She writes, ". . . these peacocks seem to have mainly a decorative function which probably has to be assigned to this motif in Jativa as well." G. Öney, in her article, "The Interpretation of Frescoes in the I. Kharragan mausoleum Near Qazwin," writes: "these peacock examples belong to Seljuk palace decoration. We believe that peacocks together with pomegranate, fertility symbol, and elixir of life, symbol of eternal life, identify the palace as paradise," pp. 402-3.

displayed within two rotating square (quartile) frames. Two trines are arranged in dot configuration and a single dot above them may be a symbol of the conjunction. The choice of peacocks as planetary signs of conjunction and opposition is clearly due to the peacock's astral significance as Jupiter, sun, Mercury and moon. Moreover, peacock's symbolism as Jupiter, a lucky *(sa'd)* planet; or as sun indicating the fourth level of Paradise adheres and enhances the paradisaic meanings of this bird within a funerary context.

Another possible explanation would be if we considered these paintings as four stations of the moon within the solar year. Accepting the peacock in full fan as the sun or the moon, we can then identify the two rotating triangles (or the six-pointed star) as the lunar station *Althurayyā* (Pleiades). This station consists of six stars clustered close to each other and is also known by the name *al-Najm* (The Star) which justifies its star-like rendition. Al-Bīrūnī wrote:

> *Althurayyā* consists of six stars close to each other, very similar to a cluster of grapes. According to the Arabs they form the *clunis* of Aries, but that is wrong, because they stand on the hump of Taurus.
>
> The word is diminutive of *Tharwa,* i.e., a collection and great number of something. Some people maintain they were called so because the rain which is brought by their *Nau',* produces *Tharwa,* i.e., abundance. They are also called *Alnajm* (i.e., *The Star*) . . .
>
> The forty days during which this station disappears under the rays of the sun are, according to the Arabs, the worst and most unhealthy of the whole year . . .[146]

The two peacocks with intertwined necks could be seen as the lunar station *Alhana'a* (Geminorium) belonging to one of the winter stations. To quote from al-Bīrūnī:

> *Alhana'a (Geminorium)* consists of two bright stars in the Milky Way between Orion and the head of Gemini, distant from each other as far as the length of a whip. The one is called *Zirr* (button), the other *Maīsān* (walking along proudly); they stand on the foot of the second twin. According to Alzajjāj, *Han'a* is derived from the verb *Hana'a* i.e., to wind and twine one thing around the other, as if each of them were winding and twining around the other.

146. Abū Rayḥān al-Bīrūnī, *Āthārul-Bākīya* (390-1/1000) trans. into English by E. Sachau as *The Chronology of Ancient Nations* (London, 1879), pp. 343-4.

According to others, this name is to be understood of a third star, standing behind their middle, which gives them the appearance of an *inclined* neck.[147]

The representation of *Alhana'a's* two stars as peacocks may be explained by the fact that Gemini is identified with domestic fowls and birds that can be tamed.[148]

The two rotating squares may conform to the shape of the eight stars belonging to the lunar station *Alnā'a'im:*

Alnā'a'im (Sagittarii) consists of eight stars, four of them lying in the *Milky Way* in a square, which are the *Descending Ostriches,* descending to the water, which is the *Milky Way;* and four of them lying outside the *Milky Way,* also in a square, which are the *Ascending Ostriches,* ascending and returning from the water.[149]

The two confronting peacocks or peafowls could, therefore, signify the lunar station *Alzubana* (Librae):

Alzubana (Librae) consists of two brilliant stars, separated from each other as far as five yards. ... The word is also derived from *zabana* (i.e., *to push*), as if one of them were being *pushed* away from the other, not united with it.[150]

The symbolism of *Alzubana* may be due to the fact that birds are one of Libra's identifying signs.[151]

Althurayyā is one of the stations of the fall season; *Alhana'a* belongs to the winter, *Alnā'a'im* to the summer, and *Alzubana* to the spring. All four stations are *sa'd,* that is lucky and of good omen.

So what we may have are four stations of the moon within the solar year. Each station signifies a season and is also lucky *(sa'd).* Therefore, the medallions represent the cycle of life on earth caused by the motion of the heavenly bodies. The problem is that the representation of *Alzubana* (a spring station) follows rather than precedes *Alnā'a'im* (a summer

147. *Ibid.,* pp. 344-5.
148. *Elements of the Art of Astrology,* p. 224.
149. *The Chronology of Ancient Nations,* p. 348. A drawing of Alna'ā'im's physical configuration from the sixth century of Hijra has the shape of two rotating squares (see *Yavāqīt al-'Ulūm wa Darārī al-Nujūm,* ed. M.T. Dānishpazhūh (Tehrān, 1966), p. 237.
150. *The Chronology of Ancient Nations,* p. 347.
151. *Elements of the Art of Astrology,* p. 224.

station). This may of course be due to a desire for creating a balanced composition where animal (peacock) and geometric medallions alternate at regular intervals.

Whether any of these theories will eventually be proven correct remains to be seen. It is important to note again that the peacock was chosen as the main character of this scheme because of its paradisaic symbolism. Above all the meaning of the peacock as the sun which is the fourth level of the heavens and the Paradise of the devout makes its choice for a tomb very fitting.

The Gunbad as a Shrine

Like a groom she had him prepared and to dust he was delivered.
(Until) only the wind remained.
From the dust of his grave a mighty gunbad she erected,
and a house of pilgrimage that was made.[152]

In Islam, in spite of the polemics against veneration of the dead, the tombs of sufis and saints have always been sites of pilgrimages and objects of veneration. Most medieval accounts of travellers mention pilgrimages to the tombs of holy personages. Nāṣir-i Khusrau, for example, speaks of making a pilgrimage to the tomb of Sheikh Bāyazīd Basṭāmī.[153] We learn in *Tārīkh-i Qumm* that those who visit the tomb of Fāṭima are destined for Paradise.[154] The mystic al-Hujwīrī writes that, "one of the rules of travel that a dervish must observe is to visit ... the tomb of a saint; otherwise his journey will be faulty."[155]

Most rulers of Islam visited tombs of holy personages. For example, Malik Shāh visited the tombs of shi'ite Imāms Mūsā al-Kāẓim and Muḥammad al-Jawād[156] and Niẓām al-Mulk visited the tomb of Ibn Ḥanbal in 1086.[157]

Contrary to early Islam's protestations against prayers at

152. Niẓāmī, *Khusrau wa Shīrīn*, ed. V. Dastgardī (Tehrān, 1936), p. 94.

برسم مهترانش حله بربست بخاکش داد وآمد باد دردست
زخاکش گنبدی عالی برافراخت وزان گنبد زیارتخانه ای ساخت

153. *Safar-nāma* (437-444/1052-1066) ed. N. Vazīnpūr (Tehrān, 1971), p. 3.
154. P. 215 and 225.
155. *The Kashf al-Maḥjūb*, p. 345.
156. G. Le Strange, *Baghdad During the 'Abbāsid Caliphate* (N.Y., 1972), p. 162.
157. *Ibid.*, p. 159.

tombs and pilgrimages to them, the veneration of tombs became an important aspect of the Islamic cult of the dead. This is indicated by the existence of an extensive body of literature on the lives of the saints with passages explaining the when, where and how of venerating a tomb. Prominent among them are *Tārīkh-i Mullā Zāda, Qandiyya, Maqāṣid al-Iqbal al-Sulṭāniyya,* and *Rauḍat al-Junān wa Junnat al-Junān.*[158] Introductory passages of some history books such as *Tārīkh-i Nishāpūr* also contain passages on the same subject.[159]

To show how important the veneration of tombs had become I would like to quote a passage from Samarqandī's *al-Sav'vād-al-A'zam:*

> It is said that anyone who passes a cemetery and does not pray for the dead (he will compel) the dead to ask from one another: "this man who passed (by our grave), was he a Muslim?"[160]

And:

> Prayers will benefit the living and comfort the dead. Anyone who says: prayers will not benefit the dead is a Mu'tazallī and accursed.[161]

Al-Ghazālī Ṭūsī (d. 505/1111) wrote:

> It is said that anyone who often thinks of death and visits cemeteries will find his own tomb to be a meadow of Paradise. And those who are negligent (of this ritual) will find (their tombs) to be caverns of hell.[162]

Veneration of tombs was, in fact, so important that at times they were circumambulated and this circumambu-

158. Aḥmad ibn Maḥmūd-i Mullā Zāda-yi Bukhārā'ī, *Tārīkh-i Mullā Zāda* (First half of 9/15th century), ed. 'A.G. Ma'ānī (Tehrān, 1960); Aṣīl al-Dīn 'Abdallāh-i Vā'iz, *Maqāṣid al-Iqbāl-i Sultāniyeh* (9/15th century), ed. M. Harawī (Tehrān, 1971); for *Qandiyya* cf. W. Bartold, *Turkestan Down to the Mongol Invasion,* E.J.W. Gibb Memorial, New Series (London, 1958), p. 15.
159. For full references to *Tārīkh-i Nishāpūr,* see n. 33.
160. P. 222.

درخبراست که هر که برگورستان بگذرد وآن مردگانرا دعا نکند.` مردگان
با یکدیگر کویند: این مرد که بر ما گذشت مسلمان بود؟

161. *Ibid.,* p. 66.

دعا کردن هم مردگانرا منفعت است وهم مردگانرا را راحت. هر که گوید که
مردگانرا را دعا منفعت نکند او معتزلی وملعون باشد

162. *Naṣīḥat al-Mulūk,* ed. J. Homaylī (Tehrān, 1972), p. 375.

در خبراست که هر که از مرك وگورستان یادکند گور خویش مرغزاری یابداز
مرغزاری بهشت و هر که از وی غافل باشد غاری یابد از غارهای دوزخ

lation was sometimes considered a substitute for the *ṭawāf.* Abul-ʻAlā, on the occasion of the death of two ʻAlīds, had said that, "two *takbīrs* in front of your grave are considered equal to the *ʻumra* (small pilgrimage) and the *ṭawāf* around the Ka'ba."[163] On the death of Ja'far of Barmekides, Ibn Khallīkān quotes the poet Abd al-Ṣamad al-Rakashī as saying:

> By Allah! Were it not through the fear of informers, and of the Khalif's eye which sleepeth not, we should walk around thy Gibbet (as round the Ka'ba), and kiss it as men kiss the sacred stone.[164]

Abū Sa'īd (967/1049) told his disciples to visit and circumambulate the tomb of Abul-Faḍl Ḥasan at Sarakhs and forego *hajj.*[165] Veneration of tombs was, in fact, a means of obtaining help from the saints and the holy. Goldziher writes:

> A number of legends express the confidence of the people that saints whose graves were visited in times of utter distress will lend help by extraordinary means. Even the remission of debts may be obtained by the pious through the intercession of the saint whose *qubbah* he visits reverently.[166]

The graves of saints were visited at times of calamity, sickness, drought, pestilence and war. In fact, "once when the Medinans faced starvation because of lack of rain, 'A'isha advised them to make an opening towards the sky on the grave of the Prophet. Thus the sacred grave was brought into direct contact with the angry heavens."[167]

Goldziher has rightly observed that, "In ancient Islam an insurmountable barrier divides an infinite and unapproachable Godhead from weak and finite humanity. . . ."[168] But with the emergence of the cults of saints this Godhead became approachable. The veneration of the saint allowed a kind of mediation between the ordinary man and the supreme God. This mediation was made possible because

163. Ignaz Goldziher, "Veneration of Saints in Islam," in *Muslim Studies,* 2 vols, ed. by S.M. Stern, trans. from German by C.R. Barber and S.M. Stern (N.Y., 1971), II:287.
164. *Wafiyāt al-A'yān,* I:314.
165. Reynold A. Nicholson, *Studies in Islamic Mysticism* (Cambridge, 1967), p. 62.
166. "Veneration of Saints in Islam," p. 282.
167. *Ibid.,* p. 285.
168. *Ibid.,* p. 255.

saints had godly and moral attributes. A story about the Transoxianan Sheikh Abul-'Abbās Aḥmad ibn Muḥammad al-Qaṣṣāb as narrated by al-Hujwīrī reveals this fact clearly:

> One day a camel was going through the market-place at Āmul, which is always muddy. The camel fell and broke its leg. While the lad in charge of it was lamenting and lifting his hands to implore the help of God, and the people were about to take the load off its back, the Shaykh passed by, and asked what was the matter. On being informed, he seized the camel's bridle and turned his face to the sky and said: 'O Lord! Make the leg of this camel whole. If thou wilt not do so, why hast thou let my heart be melted by the tears of a lad?' The camel immediately got up and went on its way.[169]

Here we see that the saint is an extension of God and man, and serves as an intermediary between the two.

The saintly attributes in conjunction with the sacred and inviolate qualities of the tomb provided a strong impetus for treating the tombs of saints as shrines.

As it turned out, even the secular tombs came to be treated as shrines. The presence of mihrabs in so many secular tomb structures ('Alī, Kharrāqān II,'Alawīyyān) indicate that these gunbads were used for prayers and were thus treated as shrines or chapels. Muḥammad ibn Ibrāhīm tells us that the tomb structure of Malik Tūrān Shāh ibn Qara Arslān Beg, a Saljūq ruler of Kirmān, was a site of pilgrimage by all people from near and far.[170] An interesting example is the tomb of Oljeitu at Sulṭāniyya. After Oljeitu's conversion from sunnism to shi'ism, he had intended to transport the bodies of the shi'ite martyrs 'Alī and Ḥusain to his own tomb at Sulṭāniyya.[171] If this plan had been executed, his tomb would have become the very center of shi'ite pilgrimage.

169. *The Kashf al-Maḥjūb*, pp. 161-162.

170. *Tārīkh-i Saljūqiyān wa Ghuzz dar Kirmān* [This book covers the history of Saljūqs from 467-719/1074-1319 and is based upon the work of the Saljūq chronicler Afḍal al-Dīn Abū Ḥāmid Kirmānī (d.c. 615/1218)], ed. B. Pārīzī (Tehrān, 1964), pp. 27-8.

171. Donald N. Wilber, *The Architecture of Islamic Iran: The Il-Khānid Period*, (N.Y., 1969), p. 139.

The Socio-Political Significance of the Tomb Tower

The symbolism of the tomb structure went beyond its sacred aspects; it also encompassed a broad spectrum of socio-political considerations. On the most basic level, the building of a funerary structure reflected the rank and social status of its patron. The greater the importance of the patron, the more prestigious was the tomb tower. The impressive height of the Gunbad-i Qābūs clearly matched the political rank of its patron and occupant, Qābūs ibn Wushmgīr. Bunākatī's description of the tomb tower of Ghāzān Khān (c. 1295-1305) relates the role of the tower's size with the expression of power and prestige:

> the people are in wonder (looking) at the tomb of the ruler of the land, (thinking) whether it is a ladder (reaching) to the heaven.[172]

The point is most expressly stated by Muḥammad ibn Aḥmad ibn Abī Bakr al-Maqdisī (b. 334/946) in his book, *Aḥsan al-Taqāsīm fī Ma'rafat al-Aqālīm.* He wrote:

> Behold the Dailamite kings (i.e. the Būyids) at Rayy, who build over their tombs lofty domes (qibah 'Alīyya), which they construct with all their zeal and erect to their utmost ability, lest they decay while those who are under kings build smaller domes.[173]

Since the funerary structures were built in the ruler's lifetime and conveyed such a significant message of his status, national rulers such as Qābūs, Sanjar, Ghāzān and

172. Cf. n. 41.
173. Ed. M.J. de Goeje (Leiden, 1877), p. 210. Translation from V. Minorsky, "Geographical Factors in Persian Art," in *Iranica, Twenty Articles* (Tehrān, 1964), p. 44.

Oljeitu relegated a great deal of the state's funds and available labor force to the construction of their mausolea. Waṣṣaf (d. 698/1299) reports that 14,400 workmen were busy at the construction of the tomb of Ghāzān Khān (c. 1295-1305) at Ghāzāniyya. There were also foreign engineers and workmen among the builders. In fact, he writes that fifty Armenian and Georgian workmen were killed when the dome of the structure collapsed in A.D. 1305. Some of the construction material was brought from Rūm (Byzantium). The decoration of the tomb's dome involved the use of 300 *man* (a unit of weight equal to approximately 40 pounds) of lapis lazuli *(lājwardī)*. The interior was adorned with golden and silver candlesticks and lamps *(qandīls)*.[174] In fact, the structure was important enough that Ghāzān Khān took charge of its design on several occasions, according to the historian Rashīd al-Dīn.[175] Equally lavish was the tomb of Sulṭān Muḥammad Khudābandeh (Oljeitu). The interior of this structure was so adorned with golden objects that it looked like a treasury.[176] According to historian Muḥammad ibn Aḥmad Nasavī, Sulṭān Jalāl al-Din Mankuburnī of Khāwrazmshāhs (617-28/1220-31) built a madrasa in Iṣfahān for the burial of his father's remains. He gave 30,000 dīnārs to begin construction of the medresseh and asked his governor of Iraq to pay the remainder from the state treasury.[177]

174. *Tārīkh-i Waṣṣāf*, pp. 229-230.

175. *Jāmī al-Tawārīkh*, 2:933.

176. Ḥāfiẓ Abrū (d. 833/1430), *Dhīl-i Jāmī al-Tawārīkh-i Rashīdī*, ed. K. Bayānī (Tehrān, 1971), p. 120.

... ومدفون گشت وچندان زر وزیور وکمر ومرصعات در آن گورخانه بکار بردند که
کفتی مکر گنج خانه ایست.

177. *Sīrat al-Sulṭān Jalāl al-Dīn Mankuburnī*, ed. H.A. Ḥamdī (Cairo, 1953), pp. 311-12. An anonymous Persian translation of this text was made in 7/14th century. See *Sīrat-i Sulṭān Jalāl al-Dīn-i Mankuburnī*, ed. M. Minuvi (Tehrān, 1965), p. 207, note 2. The passage quoted above does not appear in the Persian translation of the text.

ومنها أن السلطان الكبير كان مدفونا بالجزيرة على ما سبق من ذكر وفاته ورده
ودبعة حياته، فسنح للسلطان وهو محاصر خلاط ان يبني له مدرسة باصفهان فينقل
اليها تابوته من الجزيرة فسير مقرب الدين مهتر مهتران - وكان مقدم الفراشة -
الى اصفهان، وهو الذي تولى غسل السلطان الكبير ليبني بها مدرسة فيها قبة
للتابوت يحتوي على سائر بيوت المرافق مثل بيت الشاب، وبيت الفرس وبيت الطشت
وبيت الركاب وغيرها واصحبه ثلاثين ألف دينار للشروع في عمارتها. وتقدم الى
الوزير بالعراق باطلاق ما يحتاج اليه تمام العمارة من وجوه الديوان، وان يستعمل
لها آلات الذهب من الشمعدان والطشت والإبريق، وان تقام بالباب فرس النوبة بالطوف
والسحت والسرفسار. فسار المقرب الى اصفهان وشرع في العمارة ووصلتُ اليها بعد
اربعة اشهر، فوجدتها قد طلع بنيانها قدر قامة سيرة السلطان جلال الدين
منكبرني.

State funds were also used for the construction of a tomb structure ordered by Sulṭān Sanjar (511-552/1118-1157) for one of his *vizīrs*.[178] Likewise Shāh Shujā' of the Muẓaffarids (765-786/1364-1384) spent 2000,000 dinars on a building program in Mecca which included his own mausoleum.[179]

The erection of a dome over a tomb structure was another visible indication of great honor, prestige and social importance. Historically, the erection of a dome had always played a significant role in the political rituals of Islamic communities. The dome was a focal point of veneration, honor and political clout. The roots of this tradition can be easily traced back to pre-Islamic Arabia, Iran, and the Byzantine civilizations. H. Lammens has shown that among the pre-Islamic Arabs the dome *(qubba)* signified a high social and political standing.[180] In Sassanian Iran the imperial symbolism of the dome is evident from a salver showing a domed cube bearing the winged crown of the Sassanian emperor (fig. 38).[181]

38. *Detail of the central motif of a Sassanian salver, Iran. 6-7th. century A.D. After a photo in Erdmann.*

178. Muḥammad al-Bundārī al-Iṣfahani, *Kitāb Tārīkh Dūlat Āl-e Saljūq* (written 623/1224), (Cairo, 1900), p. 250.
179. Minorsky, "Geographical Factors in Persian Art," p. 49.
180. "Le culte des bétyles et les processions religieuse chez les arabes preislamites," *Bulletin de l'Institut Francais d'Archeologie Orientale de Caire,* XVII (1920), p. 63ff.
181. Grabar, "The Islamic Dome, Some Considerations," p. 197, fig. 8.

Later, within the Islamic world, the evidence on the function of the dome is extensive. Abu'l-Qāsim Muḥammad ibn Ḥawqal (active 4/10th-11th century) reports that the Khāqān of the Caspian Sea has a throne above which is a golden dome. This domed throne was the symbol of the ruler during his absences.[182] The dome has always been an important feature of *maqṣūra,* the royal space of the mosque.[183] Sauvaget has proposed that the domed room in Medina was a throne room.[184] Grabar has pointed out that, "the dome in front of the mihrab served to emphasize the place of the ruler and should be related to palace architecture" and that "in their secular uses, domes served to emphasize places honored by royal presence."[185] Similarly, Maqrizī's accounts of the dome's royal function in Fatimid Egypt are numerous and have been summarized by M. Canard in his article, "Le cérémonial fatimide et le cérémonial byzantin."[186]

Clearly, the presence of the dome over tombs was partly to indicate high rank, honor and prestige; and this was derived from the royal function of the dome in palace architecture. The poet Aḥmad ibn Ḥusaīn al-Mutanabbī (b. 354/965) reveals the royal and honorific symbolism of the dome in funerary architecture in a poem written on the occasion of the death of the mother of Saīf al-Daula of the Būyids.

> You passed and did not see evil days
> which spirit rejoices to see at an end.
> A dome of honor was arched over you
> for your son is a perfect high king.[187]

The patronage of the tomb reveals another aspect of its social and political significance. All sources agree that the building of a tomb was a significant act of patronage. Especially since the grave was viewed as a sacred and inviolate place, a *ḥarim* and a religious sanctuary.[188] Its construction

182. *Kitāb Ṣūrat al-Arḍ,* ed. and trans by J. Sho'ār (Tehrān, 1966), p. 136.
183. Grabar, "The Islamic Dome, Some Considerations," p. 195.
184. *Ibid.*
185. *Ibid.,* p. 197.
186. *Byzantion,* XXI (1951), pp. 355ff.
187. *Poems From the Dīwān of Al-Mutanabbī,* translated with notes by A. Wormhoudt (Oxford, 1968), p. 3.
188. See "On the Veneration of the Dead," p. 214ff.

commemorated and preserved the name of its builder for posterity. The foundation inscriptions further insured the patrons against the misappropriation of the structure by others[189] and commemorated their names in a most favorable light. As Niẓām al-Mulk points out in his *Siāsat-nāma* about patronage of buildings and public works: "By such action his name will be remembered and he will receive the reward of that action in the next world and prayers for his well-being will continually be offered."[190] This shows that the political gain for patronage was indeed very significant. To this end, the *Amīr* of Nishāpūr built a cupola over the tomb of Imām Riḍā in the 12th century;[191] or *Amīr* 'Alam al-Dīn Qayṣar built a mausoleum for the mystic poet Rūmī with the aid of grants from the treasury.[192] Another example is the tomb of Chihil-Dukhtarān at Dāmghān built by *Amīr* Abū Shujā' Asfār for a *pīr* of Isfahan.

Another sure way of preserving one's name as a beneficient patron was through the *waqf* which would bequeath the structure for pious uses and place it under the directorship of the Muslim clergy. Seyyid 'Alī Mar'ashī, ruler of Māzandarān, erected a gunbad, tomb, college, and library in the seventh century of Hijra and bestowed endowments for its upkeep.[193] Likewise, Ḥasan ibn Zayd ordered the construction of a tomb and bestowed gardens, farms, baths and shops in Āmul as *waqf* to pay for its upkeep.[194]

Burials next to the tomb of holy personages or even within their tombs also elevated the patron to a position of semisainthood and gave to the rule of his dynasty a sense of religious legitimacy. Examples include Mu'izz al-Daula (d. 356/967) of the Būyids who was buried in a *turba* near the tombs of Imāms Mūsā al-Kāẓim and Muḥammad al-Jawād,[195]

189. J.M. Rogers, "Waqf and Patronage in Seljuk Anatolia," *Anatolian Studies*, XXVI (1976), p. 86.
190. *Ibid.*, p. 75.
191. Raḥatu's-Ṣudūr, p. 94.
192. "Waqf and Patronage," p. 89.
193. H.L. Rabino di Borgomale, *Māzandarān and Āstārābād* (London, 1928), p. 38 and Muḥammad ibn Ḥasan ibn Isfandiyār, *Tārīkh-i Ṭabaristān*, ed. 'Abbās Iqbāl (Tehrān, 1941), p. 81.
194. *Māzandarān and Astarābād*, p. 34.
195. Busse, *Chalif und Groskönig*, p. 202.

and Aḍad al-Daula (d. 338/949) who was buried in the mausoleum of 'Alī ibn Abī Ṭālib.[196]

An important element in recognizing the socio-political significance of the tomb structure is its relation to its site. In many instances the mausoleum is the focal point of the cityscape or occupies a prominent position within the geographical setting. The aim, as we shall see from the source descriptions of tomb sites, was to assure the people of the ruler's ever presence, in life and in death. The tomb stood as a symbol of the ruler's immortality and was, therefore, a symbol of his political viability and permanence. Although today we do not know of the Gunbad-i Qābūs' exact relation to its original site, the tower is still an imposing figure in the Gurgān landscape and is visible from miles around. It shows the enormous presence of Qābūs for his contemporaries, not so much in death as in life, for the tomb was built during his lifetime and stood as a monument to his everlastingness. We know a great deal more about the location of the tomb of Ghāzān Khān, mainly through the writings of the Il-Khānid historian Waṣṣāf and a miniature painting (plate 22). In his city of Shenb (Ghāzāniyya), Ghāzān Khān had included a garden known as the Garden of Justice. The focal point of this Garden was his twelve-sided tomb. In line with every wall of the tomb a lofty structure was erected. These buildings included a mosque, a monastery , a Shafi'i school of theology, a hospital, an administration building, a library, an observatory, an academy of philosophy, a Hanafi school of theology, a fountain, a palace and a building of uncertain purpose.[197] Waṣṣaf continues by stating that in line with these twelve structures, they erected 1200 pairs of buildings in Shīrāz and other provinces of the kingdom.[198] The miniature, believed to have been painted before A.D. 1318, also shows the central location of Ghāzān's tomb hovering over its surround-

196. *Ibid.*, p. 203.

197. *Tārīkh-i Waṣṣāf*, p. 230. The name of the twelfth structure is missing from the text of Waṣṣāf.

198. *Ibid.*

ing buildings.[199] We can immediately gather, from Waṣṣāf's description, that the mausoleum of Ghāzān Khān was not only the center of Shenb but was also the navel of his empire. Likewise, the mausoleum of Oljeitu was the focal point of the new city of Sulṭāniyeh. Ḥāfiẓ-i Abrū mentions that the tomb was surrounded by magnificent buildings, among them a mosque, a palace, a banquet hall and an administrative hall.[200]

Mu'izz al-Daula of the Būyids was buried next to the tombs of Mūsā al-Kāẓim and Muḥammad al-Jawād.[201] We learn of the impressive position of these tombs from Ḥamdallāh-i Mustaufī al-Qazvīnī who mentions that Kāẓimiya measured six thousand paces in circumference, the center point of which was occupied by the tombs of Imāms Mūsā al-Kāẓim and Muḥammad al-Jawād.[202]

It appears that in some ways the rulers and the elite may have assigned more importance to their tombs than to their palaces. The palace was the seat of temporal power, whereas the tomb, because of its religious and divine symbolism, signified permanence, life everlasting and perpetuity. The rulers derived great political power from this religious base. It sanctioned them and their lineage, for the tomb's symbolism of permanence and continuity was in effect that of the ruler and his political state.

Last but not least the presence of peacocks at Kharraqān I or in the funerary textiles of Islam (fig. 31) is a further indication of high rank for the tomb's occupant either from a religious or a political standpoint. The peacock adhered by the virtue of its beauty, paradisiac and planetary symbolism a quality of excellence, high lineage and royalty to the tomb.

The eminence of Sheikh Abū Naṣr Sarrāj was attested in his surname, "The Peacock of the Poor."[203] Likewise, Abul-

199. Wilber, *The Il-Khānid Period*, p. 125.
200. *Dhayl-i Jāmi' al-Tawārīkh-i Rashīdī*, p. 68.
201. Busse, p. 202.
202. Cited in Le Strange, *Baghdad*, p. 162.
203. *The Kashf al-Maḥjūb*, p. 323.

Qāsim al-Junayd was called the "Peacock of the Divines."[204] Ibn Khallīkān refers to the chief of the Qur'ān readers as *Ṭāwūs* (Peacock) of the Qur'ān readers.[205] The poet Manūchihrī Dāmghānī pays tribute to and honors the poet 'Unṣurī Balkhī by calling him the "Peacock of Eloquence."[206] And after the Mystic Abūl Khayr al-Ḥusaīn (d. 420/1029) was buried in Abarqū the site was thereafter identified as the "Tomb of the Peacock."[207]

The peacock is therefore associated with the best and the most exalted. The poet Ẓāhir Fāryābī (d. 598/1202) calls the peacock the sulṭān of the good and the righteous.[208] It is indeed strange that the same bird that stands for the fall of Adam and Eve can also represent the ultimate of righteousness. Thus even the Prophet Muḥammad came to be described as a Peacock on the Tree of Certainty.[209]

It is therefore no wonder that the peacock appears alongside the image of the enthroned ruler (plate 23).[210] Clearly as a sign of excellence and superflous qualities it symbolizes the majesty of the king. This king-peacock association is partly derived from the astral (sun or light) significance of the ruler which is recognized in the figure of the peacock as a sun symbol.[211] The indentification of the king with the peacock is brought across in a poem of Āthīr al-Dīn-i Akhsīkatī (d. 560/1160) panegyrizing Sulṭān Arslān ibn Ṭughril of the Saljūqs. He writes:

> (The king is) in singularity a sīmurgh *('anqā')* and in speed a falcon,
> in sagacity a *hud hud* and in imperial glory a peacock.[212]

204. *Ibid.*, p. 189.
205. *Wafiyāt al-A'yān*, I:118.
206. *Dīvān*, p. 109.
207. Zarkūb Shīrāzī (d. 789/1387), *Shīrāz-nāma*, ed. V. Javādī (Tehrān, 1971), p. 118.
208. *Dīvān*, ed. T. Bīnish (Tehrān, 1958), p. 18.
209. A.J. Wensinck, "The Tree and Bird as Cosmological Symbols in Western Asia," p. 38.
210. For more examples of peacocks in throne scenes see Otto-Dorn, "Das Seldschukische Thronbild," *Persica*, X (1982), plates 1a, 16 and page 173, Esin Atil, *Ceramics from the World of Islam* (Washington, D.C., 1973), plate 35; D.S. Rice, "Inlaid Bronzes from the Workshop of Ahmed al-Dhaki al-Mawsili," *Ars Orientalis*, II (1957), fig. 13 and Otto-Dorn, *Kunst Des Islam* (Baden-Baden, 1964), plate 138.
211. See notes 127-135 and their accompanying texts.
212. *Dīvān*, ed. R.H. Farrukh (Tehrān, 1958), p. 132.

Nāṣir al-Dīn-i Munshī Kirmānī the author of *Samṭ al-Ulā lil-Ḥadrat al-Ulīyā* describes the death of ruler Turkān Khātūn as the "falling of the peacock's feathers."[213]

According to the anonymous author of *Baḥr al-Favā'id* (written 6/12 century) the figure of the peacock in dreams is interpreted to be a Persian king.[214] Likewise, al-Damīrī reports that he who dreams that he is in the company of a peacock is in the company of the Persian king.[215]

It is therefore apparent that the representation of peacocks in tombs or on textiles also strengthened and enhanced the socio-political significance of its occupant or intended occupant.

213. P. 49.
214. Ed. M.T. Dānishpazhūh (Tehrān, 1966), p. 421.
215. *Ḥayāt al-Ḥayawān al-Kubrā,* 1:655.

Appendix

The desire to relate the tomb to Paradise or to imbue it with paradisiac qualities is also evident in the association of the grave with water, a paradisaic attribute, or to the color white, which is a symbol of purity, sainthood and devotion to God.

The early Arabs usually prayed for water and rain over the tomb so as to give it a trait of Paradise. Furthermore, the fertility, prosperity and the productivity recognized in water must have assured the deceased of resurrection. The poet al-Mutanabbī for example, asks that the morning rains shower the grave of the mother of Saīf al-Daula of the Būyids. He writes:

> Your grave watered with the morning rain, a hint of the hand generous in giving.[216]

Ibn Khallikān reports that the following elegy was composed for the death of the Imām Malik of Medina (d. 183/795), by Muḥammad ibn al-Sarrāj.

> May the grave which has united Malik to *al-bākī* be watered with benignant showers from the dark thunder cloud flashing its lightning.[217]

216. *Poems from the Dīwān of al-Mutanabbī,* translated with notes by A. Wormhoudt (Oxford, 1968), p. 3; Arabic text in *Sharḥ al-Dīwān al-Mutanabbī* (Beirut, 1968), pp. 203-204.
Or as A.J. Arberry translates the poem:
"May a morning cloud water your resting place in morning showers equal in bounty to your bountiful hand."
Cited in *Poems of Mutanabbī* (Cambridge, 1967), pp. 56-7.

217. *Wafīyāt al-A'yān,* II:548.

The historian Abū Naṣr ʿAbd al-Jabbār ʿUtbī (d. 427/1036) wrote on the death of *Amīr* Sabuktakīn:

> Come to Naṣr's grave and say (may) the morning showers pour continously upon it.[218]

I assume, that at times when a conflict arose between a desire to cover the tomb, so as to shadow it, and also to leave it open so as to bless it with morning showers, a compromise of sorts was reached. This is partly evident in the story of the drought stricken Medinans who were advised by ʿĀʾīsha, the last wife of the Prophet, to make an opening in the grave of the Prophet to bring his tomb in direct contact with the sky and the heavens. The theory, presumably to have been that the benignant morning showers could not help but pour upon the Prophet's grave and by extension, of course, benefit the Medinans.[219]

Another rationalization of this conflict may be seen in the belief that the apex of the dome was viewed as "The Paradise" and the source of water. An example is the story of Ḥāmid in search of Paradise who is told by the angel Gabriel that the apex of the dome is "The Paradise" and the source of the river Nile.[220]

The white washing of the tomb was another means of imbuing the structure with paradisaic qualities. A white tomb reflected the purity, spirituality and religiousity of its occupant. In Islam, similar to Christianity, the color white had strong associations with purity, goodness and devotion to God. Aḥmad-i Jām-i Zhendeh Pīl wrote in his *Miftāḥ al-Nijāt* (written 532/1138) that, "on the day of reckoning only those with white faces (i.e. those who are not guilty) are resurrected."[221] In the mystical writings of medieval Islam the color white is a sign of sainthood and the pure spirit. Al-Hujwīrī, for example, writes:

218. *Tārīkh-i Yamīnī,* translated into Persian by Sharaf-i Nāṣiḥ ibn Ẓafar al-Jurfādqānī as *Tarjuma-yi Tārīkh-i Yamīnī,* ed. J. Shoʿār (Tehrān, 1966), p. 404.
219. Goldziher, "Veneration of Saints in Islam," p. 285.
220. See note 51 and its corresponding text.
221. Ed. ʿA. Fāḍil (Tehrān, 1968), p. 114.

> On another occasion as I was sitting alone, as is my custom, beside the tomb of Shaykh Abū Sa'īd at Mihna, I saw a white pigeon fly under a cloth (futā) covering the sepulchre. I supposed that the bird had escaped from its owner, but when I looked under the the cloth nothing was to be seen. This happened again next day, and also on the third day. I was at a loss to understand it, until one night I dreamed of the saint and asked him about my experience. He answered: "That the (white) pigeon is my good conduct *(Ṣafā-yi mu'āmalāt)* and comes every day to my tomb to feast with me.[222]

Likewise in another story the author relates that the Prophet said to his companions:

> There is a man at Qarān, called 'Uways, who at resurrection with intercede for a multitude of my people, as many as the sheep of Rab'ī at Muḍār. Then turning to 'Umar and 'Alī he said: "You will see him . . . on his left side there is a white spot as large as a dirhem . . . and he has a similar spot on the palm of his hand."[223]

It is thus no wonder that the whitewashing of a tomb became a sign of its occupant's Paradise-worthy behaviour and deeds. Ibn Khallikān, for example reports that the tomb of Ṣāḥab ibn 'Ibbād in Rayy (d. 385/995) "is still kept in good order and his daughter's descendents have it whitewashed regularly."[224] Muḥammad ibn Muḥammad ibn Ṣaṣrā writes in his *al-Durra al-Mudī'a fī l-Dawla al-Ẓāhirīya,* covering the history of Damascus between 791-799/1389-1397, that:

> There was a man in my town, a tyrannical and oppressive governor, who built a beautiful mausoleum for himself, [preparing] for his death. He ornamented it, whitewashed it, and made what was necessary for it. When he died they buried him in it, and the mausoleum became black as charcol, while from his tomb a black smoke kept rising, which everyone witnessed, and accounts of it spread in all the towns.[225]

222. *The Kashf al-Maḥjūb,* p. 235.
223. *Ibid.,* p. 83.
224. *Wafīyāt al-A'yān,* I:215.
225. Edited and translated by William M. Brinner as *A Chronicle of Damascus,* 2 vols. (Berkeley, 1963), I:257.

Bibliography

Primary Sources

Ākhsīkatī, Āthīr al-Dīn (d. 560/1160). *Dīvān*. Ed. R.H. Farrukh. Tehrān, 1958.

'Alī, M.M. *A Manual of Ḥadīth*. Lahore, n.d.

Arberry, A.J. tr. *Poems of Mutanabbī*. Cambridge, 1967.

Ardibīlī, 'Ārif (b. 711/1313). *Farhād-nāma*. Ed. A. Ādhar. Tehrān, 1976.

'Aṭṭār, Farīd al-Dīn (d. 589/1193). *Illāhī-nāma*. Ed. F. Rūḥānī. Tehrān, 1972.

'Aṭṭār, Farīd al-Dīn (d. 589/1193). *Illāhī-nāma*. Ed. and tr. J.A. Boyle. Manchester, 1976.

'Aṭṭār, Farīd al-Dīn (d. 589/1193). *Khusrau-nāma*. Ed. 'A. Khunsārī. Tehrān, 1976.

'Aṭṭār, Farīd al-Dīn (d. 589/1193). *Tadhkirat al-Aūlīyā*. Ed. M. Iste'lāmī. Tehrān, 1967.

'Ayyūqī (4/10th. century). *Warqa wa Gulshah*. Ed. Dhabī Allāh Ṣafā. Tehrān, 1966.

Bahār, M. ed. *Mujmal al-Tawārīkh wa'l-Qiṣāṣ* (520/1126). Tehrān, 1959).

Bākharzī, Abūl-Mafākher Yaḥyā (8/14th. century). *Awrād al-Aḥbāb wa Fuṣūṣ al-Ādāb*. Ed. I. Afshār. Tehrān, 1966.

Al-Bīrūnī, Abū Rayḥān. *Ātharul-Bākīya* (390/1000). Tr. by E. Sachau as *The Chronology of Ancient Nations*. London, 1879.

Al-Bīrūnī, Abū Rayḥān. *The Book of Instruction in the Elements of the Art of Astrology* (420/1029). Tr. R. Wright. London, 1934.

Bunākatī, Fakhr al-Dīn Abū Sulaymān Muḥammad ibn Dāvūd (d. 730/1330). *Tārīkh-i Bunākatī.* Ed. J. Sho'ār. Tehrān, 1969.

Al-Damīrī, Kamāl al-Dīn Mūsā (d. 808/1405). *Ḥayāt al-Ḥayawān al-Kubrā.* 2 vols. Cairo, n.d.

Dānishpazhūh, M.T. ed. *Yavāqīt al-'Ulūm wa Darārī al-Nujūm* (6/12th. century). Tehrān, 1966.

Dānishpazhūh, M.T. ed. *Baḥr al-Favā'id* (7/13th. century). Tehrān, 1966.

Fāryābī, Ẓāhir al-Dīn (d. 598/1202). *Dīvān.* Ed. T. Bīnish. Tehrān, 1958.

Al-Ghazālī, Muḥammad ibn Ghazālī of Ṭūs (d. 505/1111). *Mishkāt al-Anwār.* Ed. and tr. W.H.T. Gardner. Lahore, 1952.

Al-Ghazālī, Muḥammad ibn Ghazālī of Ṭūs (d. 505/1111). *Naṣīḥat al-Mulūk.* Ed. J. Homaylī. Tehrān, 1972.

Guillaume, A. tr. *The Life of Muḥammad.* Being a translation of Ibn 'Ishāq's *Sīrat al-Nabī.* Oxford, 1970.

Gurgānī, Fakhr al-Dīn. *Vīs wa Rāmīn* (c. 446/1056). Tr. G. Morrison. New York, 1972.

Hāfiz Abrū, Shahāb al-Dīn (d. 833/1430). *Dhayl-i Jāmi' al-Tawārīkh-i Rashīdī.* Ed. K. Bayānī. Tehrān, 1971.

Al-Hujwīrī, 'Alī ibn 'Uthmān al-Jullābī (d. 469/1076). *The Kashf al-Maḥjūb.* Ed. and tr. R.A. Nicholson. E. J. W. Gibb Memorial XVII. London, 1970.

Ibn al-Balkhī (6/12th. century). *Fārs-nāma.* Ed. G. Le Strange and R.A. Nicholson. London, 1968.

Ibn Baṭṭūṭa (d. 777/1377). *Voyages d'Ibn Batoutah.* Tr. C. Defrémery and B.R. Sanguinetti. Paris, 1853-1858.

Al-Bundārī al-Iṣfahānī, Muḥammad. *Kitāb Tārīkh Daulat Āl-i Saljūq* (written 623/1224). Cairo, 1900.

Ibn Hawqal, Abūl-Qāsim Muḥammad (4/10th. century). *Surat al-Arḍ.* Tr. into Persian by J. Sho'ār. Tehrān, 1966.

Ibn al-Jauzi (d. 597/1201). *Tablīs al-Iblīs.* Ed. M. Munīr. Cairo, 1948.

Ibn al-Jauzi (d. 597/1201). "The Devil's Delusion," being a partial translation of *Tablīs al-Iblīs. Islamic Culture,* XII/4 (1938).

Al-Iṣfahānī, Abūl-Faraj (b. 284/897). *Kitāb al-Āghānī.* 20 vols. Bulāq, 1868.

Ibn Isfandīyār, Muḥammad ibn Ḥasan (7/13th. century). *Tārīkh-i Ṭabaristān.* Ed. 'A. Iqbāl. Tehrān, 1941.

Ibn Isḥāq, Muḥammad (d. 151/773). *Sīrat al-Nabī.* 2 vols. Ed. M. Al-Saqqā, I. Al-Abyārī and 'A. Shalbī. Cairo, 1955.

Ja'farī, Ja'far ibn Muḥammad ibn Ḥasan. Tārīkh-i Yazd (732/1333). Ed. I. Afshār. Tehrān, 1966.

Al-Jāḥiẓ, Abī 'Uthmān Amr ibn Baḥr (d. 254/868). *Kitāb al-Ḥayawān.* 8 vols. Ed. A. M. Hārūn. Cairo, 1949.

Al-Jājarmī, Muḥammad ibn Badr. *Mūnis al-Aḥrār fī Daqā'iq al-Ash'ār* (741/1341). 2 vols. Ed. M.S. Ṭabībī. Tehrān, 1968.

Jām-i Zhende Pīl, Aḥmad. *Miftāḥ al-Nijāt* (522/1128). Ed. 'A. Fāḍil. Tehrān, 1968.

Al-Jorfādghānī, Sharaf-i Nāṣiḥ ibn Ẓafar (7/13th. century). *Tarjuma-yi Tārīkh-i Yamīnī.* Ed. J. Sho'ār. Tehrān, 1966.

Ibn Khallikān, Aḥmad (d. 681/1282). *Wafiyāt al-A'yān.* Tr. by Baron de Slane as *Ibn Khallikān's Biographical Dictionary.* 4 vols. London, 1842-70.

Khāqānī, Afḍal al-Dīn (d. 599/1199). *Dīvān.* Ed. 'A. Rasūlī. Tehrān, 1971.

Kirmānī, Afḍal al-Dīn Abū Ḥamīd (d. c. 615/1218). *Tārīkh-i Saljūqiyān wa Ghuzz dar Kirmān.* Ed. B. Pārīzī. Tehrān, 1964.

Kirmānī, Bardsīrī (7/13th. century). *Miṣbāḥ al-Arwāḥ.* Ed. B. Furūzānfar. Tehrān, 1970.

Kirmānī, Munshī (8/14th. century). *Samṭ al-Ulā Lil Haḍrat al-Aūlīyā.* Ed. 'A. Iqbāl. Tehrān, 1948.

Al-Māfarrukhī al-Iṣfahānī, Muffaḍḍal ibn Sa'd. *Tarjuma-yi Maḥāsin-i Isfahan* (421/1030). Translated into Persian by Riḍā Āwī in 729/1329. Ed. 'A. Iqbāl. Tehrān, 1949.

Al-Maqdisī, Muḥammad ibn Aḥmad ibn Abī Bakr (b. 334/946). *Aḥsan al-Taqāsīm fī Ma'rafat al-Aqālīm.* Ed. M.J. De Goeje. Leiden, 1877.

Mullā Zāda-yi Bukhārā'ī, Aḥmad ibn Maḥmūd. *Tārīkh-i Mullā Zāda* (9/15th. century). Ed. G. Ma'ānī. Tehrān, 1960.

Mustaufī, Ḥamdallāh (8/14th. century). *Tārīkh-i Guzīda*. Ed. and tr. by E.G. Browne and R.A. Nicholson. Gibb Memorial Series, 14/ 1-2. London, 1911.

Narshakhī, Ja'far ibn Muḥammad (d. 348/959). *Tārīkh-i Bukhārā*. Ed. M. Raḍawī. Tehrān, 1972.

Nasafī, 'Abd al-'Azīz ibn Muḥammad. *Kashf al-Ḥaqāyīq* (c. 680/1272). Ed. A.M. Dāmghānī. Tehrān, 1966.

Nasavī, Muḥammad ibn Aḥmad. *Sīrat Sulṭān Jalāl al-Dīn Manku-burnī (639/1241)*. Ed. H.A. Ḥamdī. Cairo, 1953.

Nāṣir-i Khusrau (b. 394/1004). *Safar-nāma* (437-444/1052-1066). Ed. N. Vazīnpūr. Tehrān, 1971.

Nishābūrī, Muḥammad ibn Salmī (4/10th. century). *Ṭabaqāt al-Ṣufiya*. Translated into Persian by 'Abdullāh ibn Muḥammad-i Anṣārī in 5/11th. century. Ed. H. Minūchehr. Tehrān, 1966.

Nishāpūrī, Abū 'Abdullāh Muḥammad ibn 'Abdullāh (d. 405/1015). *Tārīkh-i Nishāpūr*. Ed. B. Karīmī. Tehrān, 1960.

Niẓāmī, Ḥakīm (d. 590/1194). *Haft Paykar*. Ed. V. Dastgardī. Tehrān, 1936.

Niẓāmī, Ḥakīm (d. 590/1194). *Iqbāl-nāma*. Ed. V. Dastgardī. Tehrān, 1936.

Niẓāmī, Ḥakīm (d. 590/1194). *Khusrau wa Shīrīn*. Ed. V. Dastgardī. Tehrān, 1936.

Niẓāmī, Ḥakīm (d. 590/1194). *Sharaf-nāma*. Ed. V. Dastgardī, Tehrān, 1936.

Qummī, Ḥasan ibn Muḥammad ibn Ḥasan. *Tārīkh-i Qumm*. Translated from Arabic into Persian by Ḥasan ibn 'Alī ibn Ḥasan ibn 'Abd al-Malik Qummī in 805/1403. Ed. S.J. Tehrānī. Tehrān, 1934.

Ranking, G.S.A., ed. *A History of Minor Dynasties of Persia. Being an Extract From Ḥabīb-us-Sīyar of Khundamīr*. London, 1910.

Rashīd al-Dīn, Faḍl Allāh (d.716/1318). *Jāmi' al-Tawārīkh*. 2 vols. Ed. M. Bahār and M. Ramaḍānī. Tehrān, 1940.

Al-Rāwandī, Muḥammad ibn 'Alī ibn Sulaymān. *Rāḥatu's-Ṣudūr* (635/1238). Ed. M. Iqbāl. E.J.W. Gibb Memorial, II. London, 1921.

Samarqandī, Ḥakīm (4/10th. century). *Tarjuma-yi al-Sav'vād-al-A'zam.* Tr. into Persian c. 370/981. Ed. 'A. Ḥabībī. Tehrān, 1969.

Sanā'ī, Ḥakīm Abūl-Majd Majdūd (d. 547/1142). *Ḥadiqatu'L-Ḥaqīqat.* Ed. and tr. by Major J. Stephenson. New York, 1972.

Sanā'ī, Ḥakīm Abūl-Majd Majdūd (d. 547/1142). *Ṭarīq ut-Taḥqiq.* Ed. and partially tr. by Bo Utas. Lund, 1973.

Ṣaṣrā, Muḥammad ibn Muḥammad. *Al-Durra al-Mudī'a fī l-Dawla al-Ẓāhirīya* (covering the history of Damascus from 1389-1397). Ed. and tr. by M.W. Brinner as *A Chronicle of Damascus.* 2 vols. Berkeley, 1963.

Shīrāzī, Zarkūb (d. 789/1387). *Shīrāz-nāma.* Ed. V. Javādī. Tehrān, 1971.

Ṭabasī, Shams (d. 624/1227). *Dīvān.* Ed. T. Bīnish. Mashad, 1964.

The Holy Qur'ān. Tr. M.M. Pickthall. New York, 1977.

'Unṣurī Balkhī, Abūl-Qāsim Ḥasan ibn Aḥmad (d. 431/1040). *Dīvān.* Ed. D. Siyāqī. Tehrān, 1963.

Vā'iz, Asīl al-Dīn 'Abdullāh. *Maqāṣid al-Iqbāl-i Sulṭāniyeh* (9/15th. century). Ed. M. Harawī. Tehrān, 1971.

Waṣṣāf, Sharaf al-Dīn (698/1299). *Tārīkh-i Waṣṣāf.* Ed. 'A. Āyatī. Tehrān, 1967.

Wormhoudt, A., tr. *Poems From the Dīvān al-Mutanabbī.* Oxford, 1965.

Wüstenfeld, F., ed. *Kitāb Sīrat Rasūl Allāh.* Gottingen, 1859.

Al-Ya'qūbī, *Tārīkh.* Ed. M.T. Houtsma. 2 vols. Leiden, 1883.

Secondary Sources

Ackerman, P. "Textile Designs in Andarz-nāma," *A Survey of Persian Art.* Ed. A.U. Pope and P. Ackerman. 14 vols. Oxford, 1968. III-Fascicle: 29-52.

Adle, C. and Melikian-Chirvani, A.S. "Les monuments du XIe siècle du Damqan," *Studia Iranica.* I/2 (1972). 229-297.

Afshār, I. *Yādgārhā-yi Yazd.* 3 vols. Tehrān, 1966.

Afshār, I. "Two Twelve Century Gravestones of Yazd," *Studia Iranica.* 2/2 (1973). 203-210.

Almagro, M.; Caballero, J.; Zozaya, J. and Almagro, A. *Quṣayr 'Amra.* Madrid, 1975.

Ardalan, N. and Bakhtiar, L. *The Sense of Unity.* Chicago, 1975.

Atil, E. *Exhibition of 2500 Years of Persian Art.* Washington D.C., 1971.

Atil, E. *Ceramics From the World of Islam.* Washington D.C., 1973.

Azarpay, G. "The Islamic Tomb Tower, A Note on its Genesis and Significance," *Essays in Islamic Art and Architecture in Honor of Katharina Otto-Dorn.* Ed. A. Daneshvari. Malibu, 1982. 9-12.

Baer, E. *Sphinxes and Harpies.* Jeruselem, 1965.

Baer, E. "The Pila of Játiva: A Document of Secular Urban Art in Western Islam," *Kunst des Orients* VII/2 (9170-71). 142-166.

Balthrusaitis, G. *Cosmographie chrétienne dans l'art du moyen age.* Paris, 1939.

Bartold, W. *Turkestan Down to the Mongol Invasion.* E.J.W. Gibb Memorial. London, 1958.

Becker, C.H. *Christentum und Islam.* Tubingen, 1907.

Beckwith, J. *Caskets From Cordoba.* London, 1960.

Blair, S. "The Octagonal Pavilion at Natanz: A Reexamination of Early Islamic Architecture," *Muqarnas.* Ed. O. Grabar. I (1983). 69-94.

Boyce, M. *A History of Zoroastrianism.* Leiden, 1975.

Brandenburg, D. and Brüsehoff, K. *Die Seldschuken.* 1980.

Burckhardt, T. *Art of Islam.* Kent, 1976.

Busse, H. *Chalif und Grosskönig. Die Bujiden in Irak. Politik, Kultur und Wissenschaft. 945-1055.* Beirut, 1969.

Canard, M. "Le cérémonial fatimide et le cérémonial byzantine," *Byzantion.* XXI (1951). 355-420.

Corbin, H. *The Man of Light in Iranian Sufism.* Tr. by N. Pearson. Boulder, 1978.

Coste, P. *Les monuments modernes de la Perse.* Paris, 1867.

Creswell, K.A.C. *The Muslim Architecture of Egypt.* 2 vols. Oxford, 1952.

Creswell, K.A.C. *A Short Account of Early Muslim Architecture.* Beirut, 1968.

Daneshvari, A. "A Preliminary Study on the Iconography of Peacock in Medieval Islam," *Proceedings of the University of Edinburgh on Saljūq Art, 1982.* Ed. R. Hillenbrand. London, 1986.

Daneshvari, A. "Complementary Notes on the Tomb Towers of Medieval Iran. I: The Gunbad-i Kabud at Maraghe 593/1197," *Art et Sociéte dans le Monde Iranien.* Ed. by C. Adle. Paris, 1982. 287-295.

De Boer, T.J. "Nūr," *Encyclopedia of Islam.* Leiden, 1960.

Diez, E. "Principles and Types," *A Survey of Persian Art.* Ed. by A.U. Pope and P. Ackerman. 14 vols. Oxford, 1967. III: 916-929.

Dihkhudā, 'A. A. *Farhang-i Dihkhudā.* Tehrān, 1955ff.

Dimand, M. *A Handbook of Muḥammadan Art.* New York, 1958.

Dury, C.J. *The Art of Islam. New York, 1970.*

Erdman, K. *Iranische Kunst.* Berlin, 1967.

Esin, E. *Mecca and Medina.* New York, 1963.

Esin, E. "Al-Qubbah al-Turkiyyah: An Essay on the Origins of the Architecture Form of the Islamic Turkish Funerary Monument," *Atti del Terzo Congresso di Studi Arabi e Islamici, Ravello.* Naples, 1967. 281-313.

Ettinghausen, R. *From Byzantium to Sassanian Iran and the Islamic World.* Leiden, 1972.

Fehérvári, G. and Bivar A.D.H. "Qobeyra 1974: Advance Report on the Third Session," *Proceedings of the Third Annual Symposium on Archeological Research in Iran.* Tehrān, 1975. 255-262.

Fehérvári, G. "Tombstone, or Miḥrāb, A Speculation?" *Islamic Art in The Metropolitan Museum of Art.* Ed. R. Ettinghausen. New York, 1972. 241-254.

Fehérvári, G. "Two Early 'Abbāsid Lustre Bowls and the Influence of Central Asia," *Oriental Art*. IX/2 (1963). 79-88.

Fehérvári, G. *Islamic Metalwork*. London, 1976.

Godard, A. "Abarkuh," *Athār-é Irān*. I/1 (1936). 47-72.

Golombek, L. "From Tamerlane to Tāj Mahal," *Essays in Islamic Art and Architecture in Honor of Katharina Otto-Dorn*. Ed. by A. Daneshvari. Malibu, 1982. 45-50.

Grabar, O. "The Umayyad Dome of the Rock in Jeruselem," *Ars Orientalis*. III (1959). 33-62.

Grabar, O. "The Islamic Dome, Some Considerations," *Journal of the Society of the Architectural Historians*. 1963. 191-198.

Grabar, O. "The Earliest Commemorative Structures, Notes and Documents," *Ars Orientalis*. IV (1966). 7-46.

Grabar, O. *The Formation of Islamic Art*. New Haven, 1973.

Goldziher, I. "On the Veneration of the Dead in Paganism and Islam," *Muslim Studies*. 2 vols. Ed. by S.M. Stern and tr. from German by C.R. Barber and S.M. Stern. Albany, 1977. 209-238.

Hamilton, R.W. *Khirbat al-Mafjar*. Oxford, 1959.

Herzfeld, E. *Geschichte der Stadt Samarra*. Berlin, 1948.

Hillenbrand, R. "Saljūq Monuments in Iran, I," *Oriental Art*. XVIII (1972). 64-77.

Hillenbrand, R. "Saljūq Monuments in Iran: II, 'The Pir' Mausoleum at Tākistān," *Iran*. X (1972). 45-55.

Hillenbrand, R. *Tomb Towers of Iran to 1550*. Unpublished Dissertation. 2 vols. Oxford, 1974.

Holt, E.I. "A Thousand Year Old Peacock," *Bulletin of the Los Angeles County Museum of Art*. 16/2 (1964). 11-14.

Horrowitz, J. "Die Leschreibung eines Gemaldes Bei Mutanabbī," *Der Islam*. I (1910). 385-388.

Jenkins, M. "An Eleventh Century Woodcarving from a Cairo Numery," *Islamic Art in The Metropolitan Museum of Art*. Ed. R. Ettinghausen. New York, 1972. 227-240.

Jenkins, M. "Islamic Pottery, A Brief History," *The Metropolitan Museum of Art Bulletin.* XL/4 (1983). 1-52.

Khānlarī, Z. *Rāhnamāyi Ādabīyāt-i Fārsī.* Tehrān, 1962.

Kleiss, W. "Bericht über Erkundsfahrten in Iran im 1970," *Archaeologische Mitteilungen aus Iran.* 4 (1971). 51-111.

Kleiss, W. "Bericht über Erkundsfahrten in Iran im 1971," *Archeologische Mitteilungen aus Iran.* 5 (1972).

Kühnel, E. *The Minor Arts of Islam.* Ithaca, 1971.

Lammens, H. "Le culte des bétyles et les processions religieuse chez les Arabes preislamites," *Bulletin de L'Institut Francais d'Archeologie Orientale de Caire.* XVII (1920).

Le Strange, G. *Baghdad During the 'Abbāsid Caliphate.* New York, 1972.

Luschey-Schmeisser, I. *The Pictorial Tile Cycle of Hasht Behesht in Isfahan and its Iconographic Tradition.* Rome, 1978.

Meier, F. "The Spiritual Man in the Persian Poet 'Aṭṭār," *Spiritual Disciplines.* Tr. by R. Manheim. New York, 1970.

Melikian-Chirvani, A. "The Sufi Strain in the Art of Kashan," *Oriental Art.* 12/4 (1966). 251-258.

Meyer-Riefstahl. *The Parrish Watson Collection of Muḥammadan Potteries.* Paris, 1922.

Mc Govern, W.M. *The Early Empires of Central Asia.* Chapel Hill, 1939.

Menzel, T. "Yazīdī," *Encyclopedia of Islam.* Leiden, 1960.

Miles, G.C. "Miḥrāb and 'Anazah: A Study in Early Islamic Iconography," *Archeologica Orientalia in Memoriam Ernst Herzfeld.* Ed. by G.C. Miles. New York, 1952. 158-171.

Minorsky, V. "Vīs u Rāmīn, A Parthian Romance," *British School of Oriental and African Studies.* XI/4 (1946). Reproduced in *Iranica, Twenty Articles.* Tehrān, 1964. 151-199.

Minorsky, V. "Geographical Factors in Persian Art," *Iranica, Twenty Articles.* Tehrān, 1964.

Musil, A. *Kusejr 'Amra.* Wien, 1907.

Nicholson, R.A. *Studies in Islamic Mysticism.* Cambridge, 1967.

Öney, G. "The Interpretation of Frescoes in the I. Kharragan Mausoleum Near Qazwin," *Akten des VII Internationalen Kongresses für Iranische Kunst und Archäologie, München, 1976.* Berlin, 1979. 400-408.

Otto-Dorn, K. *L'Art de L'Islam.* Paris, 1964.

Otto-Dorn, K. "Bericht über die Grabung in Kobadabad, 1966," *Archäologischer Anzeiger.* 4 (1969). 438-506.

Otto-Dorn, K. "Figural Stone Reliefs on Seljuk Sacred Architecture in Anatolia," *Kunst des Orients.* XII/1-2 (1978-9). 103-149.

Otto-Dorn, K. "Das Seldschukische Thornbild," *Persica.* X (1982). 149-194.

Pope, A.U. *Masterpieces of Persian Art.* New York, 1945.

Pope A.U. and Ackerman, P. *A Survey of Persian Art.* 14 vols. Oxford, 1967.

Pugachenkova, G.A. *Puti Razvitiya Arkhitekturi Iuzhonogo Turkmenistana Pori Rabovlodeniya Feodalizma, Trudi Iuzhno Turkmenitanskoi Arkheol. Eksepeditsky.* VI. Moscow, 1958.

Rabino, H.L. *Māzandarān and Āstārābād.* London, 1928.

Rāghīb, Y. "Les premiers monuments funéraires de l'Islam," *Annales Islamologiques.* IX (1970). 21-36.

Rempel, L. "The mausoleum of Ismā'il The Sāmānid," *Bulletin of the Iranian Institute for Persian Art and Archeology.* 4 (1936). 198-209.

Rice, D.S. "Inlaid Bronzes From the Workshop of Ahmed al-Dhakki al-Mawsili," *Ars Orientalis.* II (1957). 283-326.

Rice, D.T. *Islamic Art.* New York, 1969.

Rogers, J.M. "Waqf and Patronage in Seljuk Anatolia," *Anatolian Studies.* XXVI (1976). 69-103.

Sauvaget, J. *La mosquée omeyyade de Médine.* Paris, 1947.

Schmidt, H. "Senmurv," *Persica.* IX (1980). 1-85.

Schroeder, E. "The Seljuk Period," *A Survey of Persian Art.* Ed. by A.U. Pope and P. Ackerman. 14 vols. Oxford, 1967. III: 981-1045.

Shepherd, D.G. "Technical Aspects of Buyid Silks," *A Survey of Persian Art.* Ed. A.U. Pope and P. Ackerman. 14 vols. Oxford, 1967. XIV: 3090-3099.

Simson, O.V. *The Sacred Fortress.* Chicago, 1948.

Smith, E.B. *The Dome.* Princeton, 1951.

Smith, R.; Bray, J.; Ezzy, W. "Marble and Stucco," *Arts of Islam.* London, 1976.

Soper, A.C. "The Dome of Heaven," *Art Bulletin.* XXIX (1947). 225-248.

Strika, V. "The Turbah of Zumurrud Khātūn in Baghdad, Some Aspects of Funerary Ideology in Islamic Art," *Annali dell' Instituto Orientali di Napoli.* 38, N.S. XXVIII (1978). 283-296.

Strika V. "La Cathedra di S. Pietro A Venezia: Note Sculla Simbologia Astrale nell'Arte Islamica," *Annali dell Instituto Orientale di Napoli.* 38/2 (1978). 1-88.

Stronach, D.B, and Cuyler Young, T., Jr. "Three Seljuq Tomb Towers," *Iran.* IV (1966). 1-20.

Swietochoski, M.L. "The Historical Background and Illustrative Character of the Metropolitan Museum's Manṭiq al-Ṭayr of 1483," *Islamic Art in The Metropolitan Museum of Art.* Ed. R. Ettinghausen. New York, 1972. 39-72.

The David Collection. Cophenhagen, 1975.

Tolstov, S.P. *Scythians of Aral Sea and Khorezm.* Moscow, 1960.

Touir, Q. "The First and Second Seasons at Heraqaleh: 1976-1977," *Al-Arabiya al-Sūrīya.* 27-28 (1977-1978). 111-130.

Ünsal, B. *Turkish Islamic Architecture.* London, 1970.

Al-Ush, Abūl-Faraj. *Musée National de Damas.* Damascus, 1976.

Wensink, A.J. "Tree and Bird as Cosmological Symbols in Western Asia," *Verhandelingen der Koninklijke Akademie van Wetenschappen Te Amsterdam.* 1921. 1-46.

Wiet, G. *Soieries Persanes.* Cairo, 1947.

Wilber, D. *The Architecture of Islamic Iran: The Il-Khanid Period.* New York, 1969.

Will, E. "La tour funéraire de la Syrie et les monuments apparentées," *Syria.* XXVI (1949). 258-312.

Wilson, P.P. *Islamic Art.* New York, 1957.

Wolska, W. *La topographie chrétienne de Cosma Indicopleustes.* Paris, 1962.

1. Saba' Banāt, Fusṭāṭ. Fatimid period. Circa A.D. 1010.

2. Sāmānid Mausoleum, Bukhārā. Sāmānid period. 10th. century A.D.

II

4. *Gunbad-i Qābūs, Gurgān. Ziyārid period. A.D. 1007. After Brandenburg.*

5. *Gunbad-i Surkh, Marāgha. Saljūq period. A.D. 1147. After Brandenburg.*

III

IV

8. *Gunbad-i 'Alī, Abarqū. Kākūyid period. A.D. 1038. After Godard.*

9. *Kharraqān I, Kharraqān. Saljūq period. A.D. 1067-8.*

VI

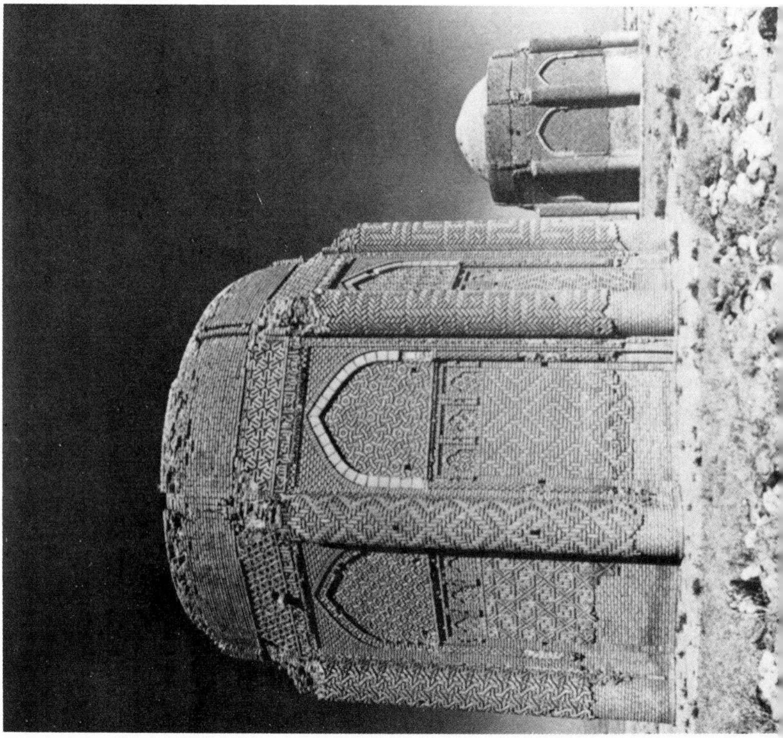

12. Burj-i Mihmāndūst, Dāmghān. Saljūq period. A.D. 1097.

13. Burj-i Ṭughril, Rayy. Saljūq period. A.D. 1139. After Pope.

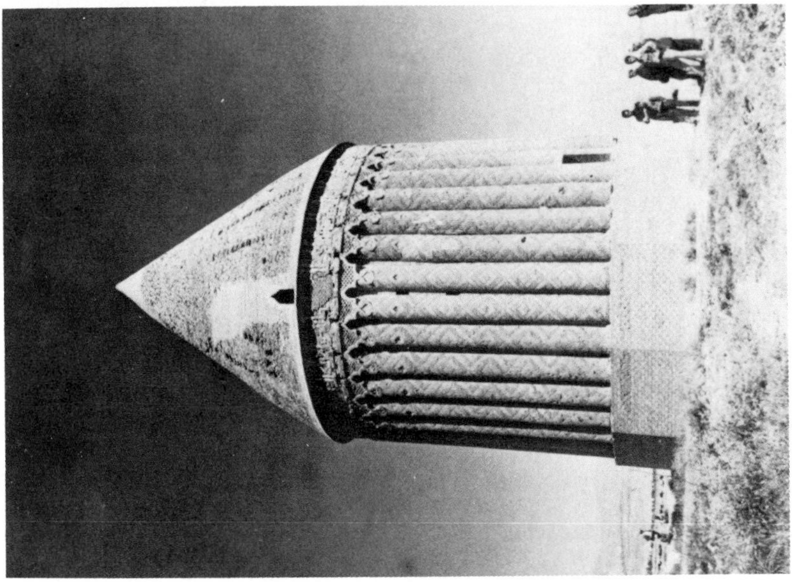

16. Burj-i Basṭām, Basṭām. Il-Khānid period. A.D. 1313. After Pope.

17. Detail of the wall of the Octagonal Pavilion, Naṭanz. Būyid period. A.D. 999. After Blair.

18. *Interior surface of the Jāmiʿ Mosque, Varāmīn. Il-Khānid period. A.D. 1322. After Pope.*

19. Interior of the dome of the Hall of Two Sisters, Alhambra Palace. Granada. 13th. century A.D. After Burckhardt.

20. *Turbah of Zumurrud Khātūn, Baghdad. 'Abbāsid period. Circa 13th. century A.D. After Strika.*

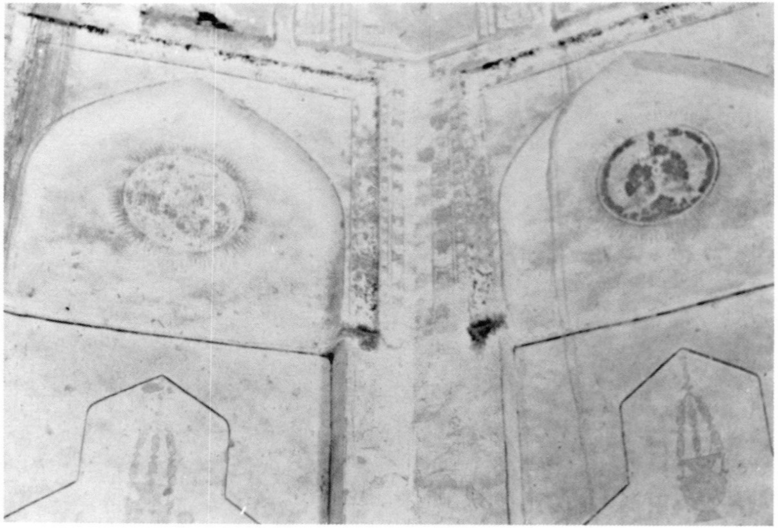

21. *Interior view of Kharraqān I, Kharraqān. Saljūq period. A.D. 1067-8.*

22. *Miniature painting of the city of Ghāzān Khān, painted before A.D. 1318. After Wilber.*

23. *Mīnā'ī bowl with enthroned ruler and peacocks. Iran. Late Saljūq period. Courtesy of the British Museum.*